The Rottweiler

OUR BEST FRIENDS

OUR BEST FRIENDS

The Rottweiler

Janice Biniok

ELDORADO INK

Produced by OTTN Publishing, Stockton, New Jersey

Eldorado Ink
PO Box 100097
Pittsburgh, PA 15233
www.eldoradoink.com

CPSIA compliance information: Batch#101909-8. For further information, contact
Eldorado Ink at info@eldoradoink.com.

First printing

1 3 5 7 9 8 6 4 2

Library of Congress Cataloging-in-Publication Data

Biniok, Janice.
    The Rottweiler / Janice Biniok.
        p. cm. — (Our best friends)
    Includes bibliographical references and index.
    ISBN 978-1-932904-64-2
    1. Rottweiler dog. I. Title.
    SF429.R7B56 2010
    636.73—dc22

                                        2009041445

Photo credits: © cynoclub/iStockphoto.com: 58, 87, 95; © Armando Frazao/iStockphoto.com:
78; © Suzann Julien/iStockphoto.com: 8; © Maciej Laska/iStockphoto.com: 35; © Tom
Lewis/iStockphoto.com: 68, 71; © Brenda McEwan/istockphoto.com: 98; © 2009
Jupiterimages Corporation: 24, 67; © Kathleen Sanderson: 90; used under license from
Shutterstock, Inc.: 3, 11, 13, 16, 18, 20, 21, 26, 28, 31, 32, 36, 41, 44, 45, 46, 54, 55, 61, 63,
64, 66, 69, 72, 73, 77, 80, 83, 84, 88, 89, 93, 99, 101, 106, all cover photos; Wikimedia
Commons: 12, 22, 81.

**For information about custom editions, special sales, or premiums,
please contact our special sales department at info@eldoradoink.com.**

TABLE OF CONTENTS

Introduction

GARY KORSGAARD, DVM

The mutually beneficial relationship between humans and animals began long before the dawn of recorded history. Archaeologists believe that humans began to capture and tame wild goats, sheep, and pigs more than 9,000 years ago. These animals were then bred for specific purposes, such as providing humans with a reliable source of food or providing furs and hides that could be used for clothing or the construction of dwellings.

Other animals had been sought for companionship and assistance even earlier. The dog, believed to be the first animal domesticated, began living and working with Stone Age humans in Europe more than 14,000 years ago. Some archaeologists believe that wild dogs and humans were drawn together because both hunted the same prey. By taming and training dogs, humans became more effective hunters. Dogs, meanwhile, enjoyed the social contact with humans and benefited from greater access to food and warm shelter. Dogs soon became beloved pets as well as trusted workers. This can be seen from the many artifacts depicting dogs that have been found at ancient sites in Asia, Europe, North America, and the Middle East.

The earliest domestic cats appeared in the Middle East about 5,000 years ago. Small wild cats were probably first attracted to human settlements because plenty of rodents could be found wherever harvested grain was stored. Cats played a useful role in hunting and killing these pests, and it is likely that grateful humans rewarded them for this assistance. Over time, these small cats gave up some of their aggressive wild behaviors and began living among humans. Cats eventually became so popular in ancient Egypt that they were believed to possess magical powers. Cat statues were placed outside homes to ward off evil spirits, and mummified cats were included in royal tombs to accompany their owners into the afterlife.

Today, few people believe that cats have supernatural powers, but most pet owners feel a magical bond with their pets, whether they are dogs, cats, hamsters, rabbits, horses, or parrots. The lives of pets and their people become inextricably intertwined, providing strong emotional and physical rewards for both humans and animals. People of all ages can benefit from the loving companionship of a pet. Not surprisingly, then, pet ownership is widespread. Recent statistics indicate that about 60 percent of all households in the United States and Canada have at least one pet, while the figure is close to 50 percent of households in the United Kingdom. For millions of people, therefore, pets truly have become their "best friends."

Finding the best animal friend can be a challenge, however. Not only are there many types of domesticated pets, but each has specific needs, characteristics, and personality traits. Even within a category of pets, such as dogs, different breeds will flourish in different surroundings and with different treatment. For example, a German Shepherd may not be the right pet for a person living in a cramped urban apartment; that person might be better off caring for a smaller dog like a Toy Poodle or Shih Tzu, or perhaps a cat. On the other hand, an active person who loves the outdoors may prefer the companion-ship of a Labrador Retriever to that of a small dog or a passive indoor pet like a goldfish or hamster.

The joys of pet ownership come with certain responsibilities. Bringing a pet into your home and your neighborhood obligates you to care for and train the pet properly. For example, a dog must be housebroken, taught to obey your commands, and trained to behave appropriately when he encounters other people or animals. Owners must also be mindful of their pet's particular nutritional and medical needs.

The purpose of the OUR BEST FRIENDS series is to provide a helpful and comprehensive introduction to pet ownership. Each book contains the basic information a prospective pet owner needs in order to choose the right pet for his or her situation and to care for that pet throughout the pet's lifetime. Training, socialization, proper nutrition, potential medical issues, and the legal responsibilities of pet ownership are thoroughly explained and discussed, and an abundance of expert tips and suggestions are offered. Whether it is a hamster, corn snake, guinea pig, or Labrador Retriever, the books in the OUR BEST FRIENDS series provide everything the reader needs to know about how to have a happy, well-adjusted, and well-behaved pet.

Rottweilers are strong, intelligent, and confident dogs that are very protective of their human families and homes. To be happy, a Rottweiler needs firm leadership, as well as lots of love and respect.

CHAPTER ONE

Is a Rottweiler Right for You?

People often describe Rottweilers as "awesome" or "fearsome." Although this first impression attracts many admirers to the breed, the Rottweiler has much more to offer than just an impressive countenance and a sense of security. Rottweilers are versatile, hard-working dogs that possess the mental and physical ability to accomplish great things.

Such potential carries with it great responsibility. The physical and temperamental characteristics of this breed require careful consideration and lifestyle changes. Not everyone is capable of caring for a Rottweiler, but those who are have an opportunity to enjoy the plentiful rewards of owning one of these powerful dogs.

Do you have what it takes to be a pet parent to a Rottweiler?

PHYSICAL CHARACTERISTICS

There is no circumventing the fact that Rottweiler ownership is demanding. This is in large part due to the size and strength of these dogs. Nobody ever said possessing such a remarkable creature would be without challenges. Before purchasing a Rottweiler, it is important to evaluate the physical characteristics of this breed and make sure one of these large dogs is right for your living situation.

SIZE: The Rottweiler is a robust canine specimen, with males reaching 24 to 27 inches (61 to 68 cm) at the shoulder, and females falling between 22 and 25 inches (56 and 63 cm) at the shoulder. This substantial frame has plenty of girth to go with its height. Adult Rottweiler males typically weigh between 95 and 135 pounds (43 and 61 kg), while adult females usually weigh between 80 and 100 pounds (36 and 45 kg).

The Rottweiler's size can create challenges. Even though these dogs naturally have a loving temperament, larger dogs can accidentally injure a small child. In particular, young, boisterous Rottweilers do not always realize their size and strength. When they try to express their affection or excitement, these dogs can easily knock little kids down like bowling pins. It is best to wait until children

FAST FACT

The reputation of the Rottweiler breed has both advantages and disadvantages. On the one hand, there is a sense of security knowing that burglars are not likely to target a home where a Rottweiler is on duty. On the other hand, you may have friends or family members who are afraid to enter your home. To win people over, be prepared to demonstrate your dog's sweet nature, excellent manners, and good training.

are big enough to hold their own in the company of a large dog before getting a Rottweiler. For the same reason, Rottweilers may be too large and strong to serve as pets for older people.

Of course, Rottweilers with the right temperament and proper training can make a fine pet for anyone, no matter the age. But attempting to integrate a Rottweiler into a home with very young children or elderly residents should be done only by those already experienced with the Rottweiler breed. Adequate training, supervision, and preventive measures are required to avoid problems.

STRUCTURE: The Rottweiler's powerful structure makes him look like the bodybuilder of the dog world, and these looks definitely aren't deceiving. This is a very strong dog! Although it will benefit a Rottweiler owner to have the physical strength to restrain such a powerhouse, it is much more important to be an effective canine leader and trainer. Mankind was given a higher intelligence than dogs, and Rottweiler owners must use that advantage. Attempts to control a Rottweiler physically, rather than mentally, will ultimately result in failure, because few humans can match a Rottweiler in physical strength and endurance.

Despite the liabilities associated with the Rottweiler's brawn, it is also a source of great pride for the breed's admirers. If you appreciate a Rottweiler's physique, it is logical to consider participating in demanding sports that will put your Rottweiler's indomitable strength to good use, such as Schutzhund ("protection dog") tests, weight pull competitions, and agility trials.

COAT APPEARANCE AND COLOR:
The Rottweiler's short, neat coat has many advantages. It is attractive, and does not easily collect dirt or become matted.

Rottweilers shed only moderately. These dogs require just five to ten minutes of brushing once a week and an occasional bath to look their best.

Unlike some dog breeds, pure-bred Rottweilers do not come in a variety of coat colors. All Rottweilers are primarily black, with contrasting markings on the muzzle, neck, eyebrows, chest, and legs. The color of these markings may vary slightly from rust to mahogany in color, but the pattern is always the same.

Rottweilers are easy to recognize because of their distinctive appearance. Unfortunately, this may subject you and your dog to "breed bias." A few highly publicized cases of errant Rottweilers have influenced public

According to the American Kennel Club's breed standard, "The ideal Rottweiler is a medium large, robust, and powerful dog, black with clearly defined rust markings. His compact and substantial build denotes great strength, agility, and endurance."

opinion about this noble breed in an unfavorable way, so be prepared for some people to react negatively when you're out in public with your Rottweiler.

TEMPERAMENT

A Rottweiler's physical power is accompanied by a strong personality. For this reason, you should consider all the facets of the Rottweiler's tem-perament to make sure this is the right breed for you.

PROTECTIVE INSTINCT: Many people are initially attracted to Rottweilers because of the protective nature of these dogs. In today's unsafe world, possessing a canine bodyguard with a daunting reputation can provide peace of mind. But this protection does not come without a price.

DOCKING A ROTTWEILER

In the United States, one physical characteristic that sets Rottweilers apart from other black-and-rust patterned dogs is its docked, or shortened, tail. According to the American Kennel Club's breed standard, a description of the ideal characteristics for Rottweilers, the dogs' tails should be amputated at the first or second tail vertebrae. This procedure is performed when a puppy is only a couple days old, so it will have been done well before you acquire a purebred dog from a breeder.

Historically, the tails of working and herding dogs were docked for practical purposes. A working dog's tail can become injured, and this damage does not heal easily and can eventually affect a dog's overall health. However, tail docking is painful for the dog, so today some American breeders opt not to perform this procedure on their puppies. Germany and several other European countries have outlawed tail docking, so Rottweilers in those places possess natural tails. As you can see from the photo below, a Rottweiler is aesthetically pleasing even without a docked tail.

Many cases of canine aggression are caused by a lack of trustworthy human leadership. If a dog cannot trust his owner to "take care of business," the dog believes he must take care of things himself— usually with his teeth! This reaction is not specific to Rottweilers; it applies to all canines.

It may seem like an advantage to own a dog that can provide protection by reputation alone. The sight of a Rottweiler can be enough to discourage potential robbers or burglars. However, you don't want to be ostracized by friends, family, neighbors and co-workers because of unfair beliefs about the danger posed by a Rottweiler. You'll need to learn how to properly introduce your dog to other people.

Because Rottweilers may initially appear serious and aloof, many people are not aware of this breed's inherently friendly disposition. Rottweilers prefer to investigate strangers with a few quick sniffs. In most cases, the dog will quickly determine a person's good intentions; then his affectionate personality can come to the surface. Think of this as, "guard duty first; socializing second." You'll be surprised how many people change their negative opinions about Rottweilers once they have met one.

Although by nature Rottweilers will attempt to protect their owners, these dogs should not be unpre-

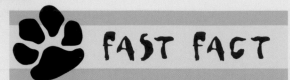

Some people make the mistake of thinking a dog with a strong personality will help them gain the confidence and assertiveness they lack, only to find out that such a dog is too much for them to handle. The truth is that an assertive, confident dog requires an assertive, confident owner!

dictably aggressive if properly trained and socialized. Your dog will understand the difference between a midnight break-in and relatives coming over for Thanksgiving dinner. However, these dogs do tend to defend their territory. It's not a good idea to keep a Rottweiler chained outdoors, as this can intensify a dog's territorial aggression. (Rottweilers prefer to be indoor pets, anyway.) Rottweilers are also known to develop the bad habit of fence-line aggression. Behaviors like barking and snarling when someone approaches your property must be addressed and eliminated early. Inappropriate aggression should never be tolerated, especially with a dog as large and potentially dangerous as a Rottweiler.

INDEPENDENT NATURE: Training is one of the things a Rottweiler owner needs to take very seriously, as the Rottweiler has his own mind and he likes to use it. This independent streak is a sign of intelligence and boldness—an admirable trait for a dog that is often expected to perform its duties without constant human direction. But this characteristic can also present challenges. Without firm, consistent leadership, the large, powerful Rottweiler can become hard to handle.

The Rottweiler is generally not considered a dog for beginners. It helps to have prior experience with dogs and dog training before bringing a Rottweiler into your life. It is also important to have an assertive personality. A Rottweiler can easily dominate a meek, submissive human. In order to control a Rottweiler, you need to have a measure of confidence. Confidence is gained through experience. Expert guidance from a professional dog trainer can also help.

Proper training will teach your dog to submit to your commands out of respect and trust. Just remember that a dog cannot learn respect and trust if you treat him unfairly or unkindly. Only positive training methods should be used with Rottweilers because, as with many independent-minded breeds, harsh physical punishments can make a Rottweiler dangerously defensive.

FAST FACT

The Rottweiler's independent nature is often associated with stubbornness, but this isn't exactly correct. Rottweilers are persistent and determined, which means they require ample firmness and consistency in training. However, these dogs are among the top ten most intelligent breeds, and will learn quickly and willingly when the proper training methods are used.

The damage done by the use of force and pain in training a Rottweiler cannot be easily corrected. Positive training methods, on the other hand, help to nurture a Rottweiler's will to please. You won't be able to trust your dog until he learns to trust and obey you.

EXERCISE AND ENERGY LEVEL: The Rottweiler isn't always a serious fellow. You might be surprised to find that beneath his stoic façade, your Rottweiler has a very playful nature. Some Rottweilers can actually be quite clownish.

A Rottweiler will have plenty of stamina for both work and play, but he should not be hyperactive, nervous, or high-strung. Properly trained Rottweilers are known for their calm nature and tendency to evaluate a situation before acting. They are quiet and reserved, personality traits that make them appropriate house pets and companions. But when excited, Rottweilers can become quite boisterous.

Young Rottweilers, in particular, enjoy playing rough, so it's important to direct their energy to appropriate activities. An overly excited Rottweiler can easily hurt someone, so discourage your pet from jumping on visitors or wrestling with humans. For the safety of everyone who comes in contact with your dog, Rottweilers must be taught at an early age to respect the personal space of humans. Without such training, a Rottweiler may become physically pushy, dominant, and disrespectful.

That said, keep in mind that these muscular, athletic animals need opportunities to use their physical gifts. Exercise is important for both mental and physical well being. In addition to a daily walk, be sure

FAST FACT

Of all the commendable traits possessed by this breed, for many people it is the Rottweiler's steadfast loyalty to their owners that inspires the most admiration.

For maximum health and happiness, Rottweilers need plenty of daily exercise.

to incorporate opportunities for good hard play into your dog's routine. An exhilarating game of fetch or a run through some agility obstacles in the back yard are excellent ways for your Rottweiler to get his fitness fix. A Rottweiler will be happiest in a home that has room for him to run, so if you're looking for an apartment pet, it's probably better to pass on this breed.

PREY DRIVE: Rottweilers are known to have a strong prey drive—a natural instinct to chase a moving target. Prey drive is what inspires a herding dog to chase and direct sheep or cattle. It is what gives a police dog the desire to pursue a suspect. Since Rottweilers excel at these canine jobs, it makes sense that this breed's prey drive is well developed.

Like other Rottweiler traits, the intensity of prey drive is an individual thing. Because Rottweilers with an extremely high prey drive may tend to "herd" people or harass other animals, it helps to consider this trait when determining whether a Rottweiler is a good match for your situation.

While there may be liabilities associated with this trait, there are also advantages. If you are interested in participating in a demanding canine sport, a high prey drive can be an exceptionally motivating force. Most Rottweilers are fully capable of learning appropriate uses for this drive, but whether or not a Rottweiler can be trusted around small pets, especially prey species like rabbits or hamsters, depends entirely on the individual dog and its upbringing.

ROTTWEILERS AND OTHER PETS

Rottweilers are often employed as all-purpose farm dogs, so obviously they can get along with other animals. Rottweilers would have become extinct long ago if they were in the habit of pursuing and killing a farmer's livestock instead of herding and protecting them. Some Rottweilers, in fact, have taken their jobs as guardians so seriously that they function as surrogate parents to orphaned horses, goats, and other critters.

That's not to say there has never been a Rottweiler that "went bad" and slaughtered all the chickens in the chicken coop. Be aware that there are some Rottweilers whose prey drive gets in the way of reasonable purpose. For this reason, you must carefully consider a dog's individual personality traits before attempting to integrate a Rottweiler into a home with other pets.

In general, Rottweilers tend to enjoy the company of other dogs, and the opportunity to expend some energy through dog-on-dog play is good for them. This large, powerful dog is best matched with dogs close to its own size, as a Rottweiler's rough-and-tumble play style may overwhelm or injure smaller canines.

There are some Rottweilers, though, that show little affinity for other dogs. In fact, the Rottweiler breed standard specifically states, "An aggressive or belligerent attitude toward other dogs should not be faulted." One of the Rottweiler's purposes, after all, was to protect livestock from other predators, including wild canines. Antagonistic behavior

FAST FACT

The serious stare of a Rottweiler can be quite unnerving. Herding dogs use their steady gaze to intimidate livestock and urge them to move, but "the eye" tends to intimidate people, too!

Male Rottweilers are generally larger and bulkier than females, with a broader, more masculine head. This size difference is specifically mentioned in the breed standard, and can clearly be seen in this photo of a male (right) and female Rottweiler.

is usually reserved for unfamiliar dogs. When raised with another dog, or properly socialized and carefully introduced to a new canine companion, many Rottweilers are open to canine friendship.

ROTTWEILERS AND CHILDREN

There are a number of reasons why Rottweilers are not recommended as pets for families with young children. The most obvious reason is the Rottweiler's size and strength. Even if a dog has an exemplary temperament, matching king-sized canines with pint-sized people can be a formula for injury, especially in light of the Rottweiler's predilection for robust physical contact.

Another problem that arises when young children and Rottweilers mix is that the shrill screams and quick movements of small children tend to excite the Rottweiler's prey drive. Even if this does not culminate in an aggressive pursuit, it can overstimulate a Rottweiler and lead to dangerously rough play.

Rottweilers are most appropriate for families with children over the age of eight. Even then, children should be taught to avoid exciting the Rottweiler. When a dog begins to play too rough, playtime should cease immediately and the dog should be ignored. Rottweilers must be taught to respect and respond to everyone in the family, including its smallest members.

THE BEST ENVIRONMENT FOR A ROTTWEILER

The Rottweiler is a very special dog breed, but unfortunately too many people base their canine preferences on all the wrong criteria.

Those who desire to own a Rottweiler as a status symbol, for example, don't understand a very important fact: If they need a Rottweiler to gain confidence and status, they already lack sufficient confidence and status to be an effective Rottweiler owner.

Those who purchase a Rottweiler for the sole purpose of protection don't realize that protection should be no more than a fringe benefit of owning a dog. Rottweilers are complicated creatures with many other facets to their personality. Your Rottweiler won't enjoy being relegated to a back yard or car lot to guard your property; he'd rather spend time with you. He'll want a job to do, to fulfill his need to be of service. And he'll appreciate a firm leader he can trust, someone to provide a calm, assertive presence in his life to make him feel secure.

The best environment for a Rottweiler, then, is one that provides for the needs of the entire dog. If you are willing to adapt your lifestyle to meet both the physical and emotional needs of a Rottweiler, you may be ready to embark on a unique canine adventure.

❧❧❧❧

A Rottweiler will not be the right dog for everyone. Consider the pros and cons carefully before you decide whether you're prepared to share your life with a Rottweiler. Even those who decide that caring for a Rottweiler is more than they can handle can't fail to admire this proud and stately breed. Those who do feel that they can handle one of these powerful dogs are in for a thrilling experience.

CHAPTER TWO

Finding the Right Rottweiler

Rottweilers represent a wonderful amalgamation of canine characteristics. Devout loyalty, physical and mental strength, an honest work ethic, playfulness, protectiveness, determination, and many other Rottweiler traits were developed through many years of selective breeding. The result is a versatile dog that can perform many different functions.

Studying the history of Rottweilers can provide interesting insights into the breed's physical and temperamental characteristics. Understanding why certain traits were valued and sought by breeders, and determining what you expect

Rottweilers make great pets because of their intelligence, loyalty, and playfulness.

from your own Rottweiler, can help you choose the right dog for you.

HISTORY OF THE ROTTWEILER

Rottweilers are believed to be descended from mastiff-type dogs employed by ancient Romans some 2,000 years ago. These dogs, called Molossers, possessed broad heads and thickly muscled bodies, traits that are still evident in the Rottweiler. Molossers were valued as war dogs and protectors, and also provided entertainment in the form of blood sports. Fighting dogs were often pitted against lions, bears, and even human gladiators in the Roman coliseums.

It is believed that Molossers themselves were descended from earlier war dogs used by the armies of Xerxes I, king of Persia, as far back as 480 B.C. These dogs may themselves have been descended from Asian war dogs known to exist prior to 1600 B.C. So the Rottweiler's ancestry is indeed a very old one.

The Molosser's courage and strength not only served it well in the arena; these qualities also made it an excellent cattle drover. This dog had the courage and physical presence necessary to drive large, obstinate bovines and to protect both the live-stock and their owners. The Molosser-type dogs used for herding were smaller and leaner than their massive war dog relatives, as excessive bulk would have detracted from the herding dogs' speed and stamina. But there is little doubt of the genetic bond between the two.

THE ROTTWEILER IN GERMANY

The Rottweiler emerged as a specific dog breed after the Romans occupied a region known as Swabia in 73 A.D. (This area includes the southern

The ancestors of today's Rottweilers were used to herd and protect cattle and other livestock. Some Rottweilers still perform this function today.

part of the modern German state of Baden-Württemberg, as well as parts of present-day Switzerland and France.) Roman settlers established an encampment along the Neckar River in Swabia, which became the town of Arae Flaviae. This town eventually earned the name Rottweil, a term that referred to the red tile roofs of the original Roman buildings.

The Roman settlers had brought cattle with them, and so, of course, they were also accompanied by droving dogs. As the town of Rottweil flourished in grain and cattle production, the Roman droving dogs were interbred with local dogs. Some of these local dogs may have had Swiss or German ancestry. Thus, the forebears of the Rottweiler breed emerged.

Dogs were commonly named after the places where they developed, as well as the purpose they served. Originally, the Rottweiler breed was often referred to as the Rottweil *metzgerhund*, which means "Rottweil butcher's dog." As both protector and herder, the Rottweiler gained a reputation as an effective tool for moving cattle to slaughter, as well as protecting the herdsmen and butchers who owned them. The size and strength of Rottweilers also made them perfectly suited for pulling carts. Dog carts were used to carry a peddler's wares or deliver milk from farms to villages.

It's hard to believe that such a useful and versatile canine almost became extinct for lack of employment, but it did. By the late nineteenth century, railway systems

This illustration from 1643 shows the German town of Rottweil, where the Rottweiler breed is said to have been developed.

provided a more efficient way to transport cattle and goods, and new laws prohibited driving cattle along the roads. As a result, the use of Rottweilers as herders and carters in Germany became outdated. Working dogs that could not earn their keep had no reason to exist, so the number of Rottweilers dropped dramatically. Only a single Rottweiler participated in a dog show held in Heilbronn, Germany, in 1882, and he was described as a "poor example of the breed." According to some accounts, by 1905 just one female Rottweiler could be found in the breed's hometown.

Fortunately, Rottweilers had migrated with their owners to other parts of Germany by that time, and the dogs were still valued by some as a source of steadfast protection. The popularity of the breed would increase again after 1910, when Rottweilers began to be employed in police work. Through breeding programs managed by German police associations, the Rottweiler population slowly grew.

Rottweilers benefited from growing public interest in purebred dogs. In the late nineteenth century and early twentieth century, stud books were established to record the lineage of dogs, breed clubs proliferated, and descriptions of ideal characteristics were formulated for individual breeds. These descriptions, known as the standard of perfection or the breed standard, became the measuring sticks by which purebred dogs would be judged.

In 1901, a breed club was formed by fanciers of Rottweilers and Leonbergers (another large, strong German working dog). The club did not last long, however. The German Rottweiler Club and the South German Rottweiler Club were both formed in 1907. The South German Rottweiler club was soon integrated into a third club, the International Rottweiler Club. Recognizing that solidarity was needed to establish true consistency in the breed, the German Rottweiler Club and the International Rottweiler Club finally merged in 1921 to form the Allgemeiner Deutscher Rottweiler Klub (ADRK). This club remains the leading German authority on the Rottweiler breed.

FAST FACT

In the early 1900s, the Rottweiler was one of four breeds of dog accepted for German police work. The others were the German Shepherd, the Doberman Pinscher, and the Airedale Terrier.

THE ROTTWEILER IN THE UNITED STATES

Rottweilers first arrived in the United States in 1929, and the breed was officially recognized by the American Kennel Club (AKC) in 1931. Still, the popularity of the Rottweiler breed in America remained surprisingly low for many years. Despite the Rottweiler's success as a police dog, and the heavy use of dogs in the military during World War II, Rottweilers remained relatively rare in the United States.

Even after a Rottweiler attained the first AKC championship for the breed in 1948, there were very few Rottweilers registered with the AKC for quite some time. The Rottweiler Club of America, which was chartered as the breed's national parent club by the American Kennel Club in 1947, became defunct within a few years due to lack of interest. It wasn't until after a new national breed club, the American Rottweiler Club (ARC), was formed in 1973 that the Rottweiler finally began to gain some

Rottweilers are often employed as police dogs because they are smart and strong.

well-deserved attention in this country. By 1997 the Rottweiler had become the second most registered AKC breed.

It's hard to say what, exactly, led to the Rottweiler's meteoric rise from obscurity to common household name, but there were a number of possible reasons. It became fashionable, and an indication of status, to own a purebred dog during the 1970s and 1980s. Also, with many people worried about crime rates, it's not surprising that Rottweilers became more desirable. Unfortunately, the explosion in interest has caused some problems for the breed. Irresponsible breeding by those only interested in capitalizing on the demand for Rottweilers led to a proliferation of physical faults, such as hip dysplasia. Some dogs were specifically bred to have vicious or aggressive dispositions, and this gave the breed an undesirable reputation that persists to this day.

Since the 1990s, the popularity of Rottweilers has slowly fallen. Today, the dog is ranked about 15th on the list of annual AKC registrations. But one thing is for sure: Rottweilers have permanently emerged from obscurity. There are very few people who have not at least heard of Rottweilers or don't know what a Rottweiler looks like.

BREED STANDARDS AND CONFORMATION

The reason it is so easy to conjure an image of a Rottweiler is because of the establishment of breed standards. The Rottweiler breed standard provides a detailed description of a "perfect" Rottweiler, and this is the criterion by which all Rottweilers are judged at conformation shows. The standard is intended to ensure that serious Rottweiler breeders always attempt to produce dogs with the same characteristics, so that the integrity of the breed is kept intact.

The International Club for Rottweilers and Leonbergers published the first Rottweiler breed standard in 1901. This standard, supposedly written by a man named Albert Krull in 1883, called for a smaller dog than the modern breed

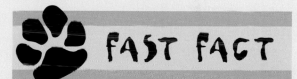

FAST FACT

One of the greatest drawbacks of the Rottweiler's explosive rise in popularity in the U.S. is the fact that there are still many unscrupulous breeders who try to produce Rottweilers with excessively sharp temperaments. These "guard" dogs can be unstable and unpredictable, so use care to select a Rottweiler with an even temperament.

standard. It also permitted color patterns that are no longer acceptable. Subsequent standards issued by the early German Rottweiler clubs addressed very different aspects of the Rottweiler. The German Rottweiler Club's standard focused on the dog's working abilities, while the International Rottweiler Club's standard was more heavily devoted to physical conformation. Eventually, when the two clubs were merged in 1921, a single German standard was developed.

When the Rottweiler was first allowed to compete in AKC conformation shows in 1935, the AKC used the German breed standard (which had, by that time, become a universal standard in Germany) as a guideline. The American Rottweiler Club drafted its own breed standard in 1979. It is slightly different from the German standard, preferring dogs that are taller, have longer legs,

and a head that is not as squarish in shape. The American breed standard has been modified slightly since 1979, but overall the appearance and characteristics of the Rottweiler breed have changed very little.

WHERE TO FIND A ROTTWEILER

If you've studied the Rottweiler breed, including its history, physical features and temperamental traits, you might be concerned about where you should look for a Rottweiler. That's because you know this is a special breed that requires careful consideration. Whether you purchase a dog from a breeder or adopt a dog from a rescue group, always scrutinize the source thoroughly.

BREEDERS: Breeders are a good source for purebred puppies, but be very careful when shopping for a Rottweiler. Breeders who purposely produce Rottweilers with aggressive

The breeder may decide which of her Rottweiler puppies is the right match for your family.

temperaments to meet the demand for "guard" dogs should be avoided. These dogs are mentally unstable and may react to situations without thinking. In this age of rampant lawsuits, you do not want to own an unpredictable, aggressive Rottweiler. So evaluate the breeder very carefully before deciding to purchase a puppy.

Always ask to see one or both of the parent dogs, because this is the best indication you will have about a puppy's future disposition. A puppy's behavior is also influenced by socialization and the environment in which it is raised. Is the puppy handled daily? Has he been exposed to children, other pets, and people other than his breeder? Is his living area kept clean? Has he had opportunities to play outside? If the answer to these questions is "yes," you'll know the breeder has put considerable effort into giving her puppies a great start in life.

Because temperament is of utmost importance in choosing a suitable Rottweiler, it is always preferable to spend a little more on a well-bred pup than to take a chance on anything less. This may mean dealing with the requirements of a purchase contract, which could include commitments to register the dog with the AKC and enroll in a socialization class, or an agreement to offer the dog back to the breeder

PROPER PAPERS

What kind of paperwork should you expect when purchasing a purebred Rottweiler from a breeder?

Registration papers—These should be prepared and ready for you to submit to the registry.

Proof of vaccinations—Puppies should have received at least one set of puppy vaccinations before they are released to new homes. Breeders who administer the vaccines themselves should be able to provide records of the date, manufacturer, and serial number of vaccines.

Puppy purchase contract—This should include health guarantees and return/refund policies.

Pedigree—This will show the puppy's family tree, and is very important if you plan to show or breed your dog.

FAST FACT

Since you'll probably have to maintain some ties to your pup's breeder, you are wise to choose your breeder as carefully as you choose a puppy. The relationship you develop with a breeder can be one of support and camaraderie, or it can become one of conflict and stress. Better to have a breeder who will be your partner in success.

before you can sell him to someone else. Although most provisions in puppy purchase contracts are reasonable, you should always read and evaluate a contract thoroughly to make sure you are comfortable with the terms.

SHELTERS AND RESCUES: If you'd rather bypass the challenging puppy stage, there is often a good supply of adult Rottweilers available for adoption through animal shelters or rescue organizations. Unlike puppies, adult dogs already display their mature personalities and are much easier to evaluate for suitability. In addition, adoption fees are reasonable and often include the cost of vaccinations and neutering or spaying.

But these "budget" dogs do not always come without some baggage. Some adoptable dogs may be unrea-

sonably shy or have behavior problems because they were abused or neglected by their previous owners. They may lack training or social skills. Some may suffer from anxiety or depression from having been abandoned by their owners.

Many Rottweilers become homeless simply because their previous owners didn't make very good Rottweiler owners, so behavioral issues that resulted from such a mismatch can often be corrected with the proper training. You'll need to

You are likely to find wonderful adult Rottweilers that need new homes at local dog shelters or rescue organizations.

evaluate each prospect individually to determine whether an adult dog is a good match for you. Avoid any Rottweiler that has an aggressive temperament unless you have experience with such a problem and feel confident you can handle it. Adoptable dogs tend to have sketchy histories, and there are not always reasonable or adequate solutions for a poorly bred dog with serious temperament flaws.

Rescue groups that specialize in Rottweilers can provide excellent advice and assistance in locating the right Rottweiler for you. You can locate Rottweiler rescue groups through a local Rottweiler club or by checking Web sites like www.rott net.net or www.petfinder.com.

OTHER SOURCES: You might see adorable Rottweiler puppies for sale at a pet store or flea market. Puppies can also be found through classified ads in the newspaper, flyers posted on a public bulletin board, or on the Internet. However, be very cautious before buying from one of these sources. If you can't evaluate a parent dog or inspect the puppy's original living conditions, there's no way to know whether a particular dog will suffer the ill effects of poor breeding or improper care. Breeders who need to advertise in newspapers or on the

FAST FACT

Anyone interested in a purebred dog can only benefit by studying the standard for that breed. Even if you are only interested in a pet-quality dog, the breed standard will give you an indication of what to expect from a good quality dog.

Internet are not always reputable or knowledgeable.

Some pet stores have good reputations for offering healthy animals for sale. Other stores put profit ahead of their dogs' health. These stores sell dogs from puppy mills—kennels that breed large numbers of dogs under terrible conditions. Puppies that come from such kennels are especially prone to serious physical and temperamental defects due to poor breeding practices and a lack of socialization.

Listen to your head, not your heart, when it comes to choosing a canine friend. Don't let the allure of a sweet puppy face spur you into an impulsive purchase. You should put at least as much thought and research into finding the right dog as you would in choosing a new car. Selecting a dog that is unhealthy or hard to train can result in financial hardship or emotional heartbreak.

You'll never regret taking extra time to find the right companion.

CHOOSING YOUR ROTTWEILER

Obtaining a Rottweiler from a source you can trust will help eliminate some of the uncertainty about getting a new dog. Still, don't be surprised if you are a little nervous about adding a Rottweiler to your family. You can erase some doubts and fears by determining what you really want in a dog, then pursuing those ideals.

SHOW OR COMPANION: If you expect your dog to mesmerize judges in the show ring, you'll have to be exceptionally choosy in your search for the perfect pup. Ideally, you will have attended many, many dog shows before deciding to get involved in the sport of canine con-

formation. This is necessary to help you learn how shows are organized. It will also give you opportunities to meet breeders who might be a good source for your future champion.

Some of the best show prospects come with plenty of strings attached. A puppy purchase contract may include provisions that give the breeder the right to take back a dog if the buyer wishes to sell or abandon him. The buyer may also be prohibited from selling the dog's offspring without the breeder's permission. Despite such restrictions, don't be surprised if there is a waiting list to obtain a quality show puppy. And if you expected to get a tiny, rolypoly puppy, you may discover that many show breeders will not part with their puppies until they are older. Puppies do not always reveal their true show potential until they are at least three to six months old.

If you're just looking for a companion, a flawed bite or unusually colored coat are not important. What's most important is that the chosen Rottweiler's personality is compatible with that of his new family.

MALE OR FEMALE: Another thing you'll want to consider is gender. Whether your dog is intended for show or as a pet, gender may affect

FAST FACT

If you have a specific purpose in mind for your Rottweiler, you can conduct a more extensive evaluation to determine your puppy's potential to succeed. The Puppy Aptitude Test (PAT) was developed by Jack and Wendy Volhard to determine the strength of various canine personality traits. You can find this test at www.volhard.com/pages/pat.php.

If you'd like your Rottweiler to compete in a particular sport or activity, such as agility trials, look for a dog whose parents were successful in that event.

the goals you have for your dog. In the Rottweiler breed, there are some rather noticeable differences between males and females. Males tend to be larger in body and bolder in temperament, traits that may appeal to you if you really want a working or sporting dog. However, these traits can also present challenges for inexperienced dog owners.

If you plan to show and breed your dog, you'll have to think about which end of the breeding process you want to be on. Raising a litter of pups can be fun, but it's also messy, demanding work. Then again, owning a stud dog presents its own challenges and responsibilities. You should thoroughly research both situations before deciding which gender is the best for you.

PUPPY OR ADULT: The decision to get either a puppy or an adult Rottweiler should not be based solely on your preference. You may be totally in love with the idea of getting an adorable Rottweiler puppy, but if you do not have the time and resources to raise a puppy, you might be better off with an older dog. Besides requiring an enormous amount of time to supervise and train them, puppies are expensive.

The cost to purchase a puppy can be significantly higher than the cost to adopt an adult dog. First year veterinary expenses are also considerably higher for puppies. Add to these the cost of collars, crates, beds and other items that may eventually need to be replaced because the puppy outgrew (or destroyed) them, and you'll realize just how pricey a cuddly canine can be.

There are certain advantages to adopting an adult Rottweiler. These dogs may already be housetrained or know basic obedience commands.

Although adult dogs may offer more value for your dollar, they do present some disadvantages. Adopting an adult dog from a shelter or rescue comes with few guarantees. The quality of a dog's breeding and the extent of his socialization and training may be completely unknown. Some adult dogs may have developed behavior issues that require expert advice to resolve, and you should make sure that any pre-existing issues are within your abilities to correct.

Fortunately, dogs are incredibly adaptable, and many adult dogs can become excellent companions with the proper training. Some of the best dogs come from humble beginnings.

EVALUATING TEMPERAMENT

So how do you know whether the Rottweiler you've found will be a treasure or a terror? There are different ways to evaluate a dog's temperament, depending on whether it's a puppy or an adult. In both cases, you can learn a lot just by asking the breeder, shelter staff, or foster home provider. These people will usually give honest observations about their canine charges.

Even though puppies are temperamentally undeveloped, they can still be evaluated for their potential personality. Dominance and submis-siveness are innate characteristics that will be evident even at a young age. A young Rottweiler that seems to dominate his littermates, plays rough and reckless, and insists on being the first in line for human attention is likely to be a challenging project even for an experienced Rottweiler owner.

On the other end of the scale, shyness and fearfulness are not appropriate traits for a Rottweiler. In fact, a Rottweiler that shows these characteristics is either mentally unstable or seriously lacking in socialization. Such a dog is very likely to bite someone out of fear, and should be adopted only by the most experienced Rottweiler handler.

The best choice, then, is a puppy that falls somewhere between these two extremes—a pup with plenty of desire to play, explore, and interact without fear, but without the self-centeredness and impulsiveness of a dominant sibling. Such a pup will grow up to have a more malleable and predictable temperament.

The personality of an adult dog should be fairly obvious. Unlike humans, dogs have no reason to be deceptive about their feelings or intentions. Still, there is one test you can do to gain an important insight into an adult dog's personality. Be sure to bring dog treats with you,

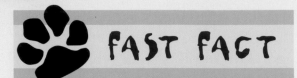

and see if you can get the dog to respond to basic obedience commands by encouraging him with the food. It doesn't matter whether or not the dog actually understands the commands; the point is to determine his "trainability." Does he look at you with intensity? Does he seem anxious to earn the rewards? If the answer to these questions is "yes," you've found a dog that should be easy to train.

EVALUATING HEALTH

When you're evaluating dogs for temperamental suitability, take some time to observe the dog's health as well. In most cases, you'll be able to tell immediately if a puppy or dog is ill. Symptoms like a runny nose, sneezing, coughing, runny eyes, and lethargy are all obvious signs that you should pass on a particular dog. Make note of less conspicuous symptoms, also. The condition of a dog's hair and coat, for example, is an excellent indicator of his general health. If a dog has a dry, flaky, oily, or dull coat, he may be suffering from physical ailments that you can't see. A bloated belly, scratching, and hair loss are all signs of parasite infestation. It doesn't hurt to check a dog's ears for signs of irritation, or take a peek at his mouth to detect any dental problems.

Handling the dog's various body parts in this way can reveal more than the dog's physical condition. You need to be able to touch your dog in order to train him and care for him. If you can't touch the dog, your veterinarian won't be able to, either.

☙☙☙

A Rottweiler with a stable temperament and good health has the versatility to fulfill many different purposes. And that is what every Rottweiler lives for—a purpose. So as you are considering the traits that appeal to you the most, think about all the possible ways you can utilize your dog's many talents!

CHAPTER THREE

Responsible Pet Ownership

The privilege of owning a Rottweiler comes with certain responsibilities. When you adopt a dog into your family, you are accepting an obligation to care for that dog. You are also accepting a duty to other people. This means abiding by all public ordinances and regulations regarding pet ownership.

It means ensuring that your dog is never a danger or even a nuisance to others. It means striving to be courteous and respectful whenever you and your dog are out in public.

Being responsible in how you handle your Rottweiler helps keep him safe and happy. It also keeps friends, relatives, acquaintances, and

Before buying a dog, be aware of your community's ordinances regarding pet ownership.

neighbors safe and happy. Although being accountable for a dog may impose some burdens, a responsible pet owner will enjoy his dog more and reap greater benefits from the canine relationship.

In some places, breed-specific legislation prohibits the ownership of certain breeds of dog within a community's limits. Due to the bad press caused by poorly bred or irresponsibly handled Rottweilers, the Rottweiler is often a target of this type of legislation. As a result, you'll need to make sure that Rottweilers are permitted in your community before you acquire one. If you are allowed to own a Rottweiler, it's very important that you be an exemplary owner. The only way to combat discriminatory breed-specific legislation is to help prove that such laws are unnecessary.

IDENTIFICATION

A new dog or puppy is not going to know his yard boundaries, and he may not respond to his new name or the "come" command at first. One important responsibility is to make sure your Rottweiler can be properly identified if he wanders off, escapes from your home or vehicle, or is taken by pet thieves.

To facilitate the return of your dog if he becomes lost or stolen, it is imperative to fit him with identification as soon as possible after you acquire him. Your Rottweiler should have a collar with an ID tag that includes his name and your home telephone number. This form of identification enables anyone who finds your pet to contact you almost immediately.

Because collars can come off, a permanent form of ID, such as tattooing or microchipping, should also be used as a backup. Your veterinarian or breeder can probably tell you

Your Rottweiler must wear a collar with an ID tag, so that if he escapes from your yard and is found, he can be returned promptly.

how to get one of these forms of identification for your Rottweiler.

Tattooed dogs are marked with a series of numbers—usually the owner's tattoo registration number or the dog's AKC registration number. Common locations for identification tattoos include the belly and the inside of the thigh.

Pet owners who are uncomfortable with tattooing can instead choose microchip implantation. In this method, a computer chip that is about the size of a grain of rice is injected under the dog's skin, between the shoulders. The chip contains data about how to contact the dog's owner. Most veterinarians and animal shelters have scanners that can detect and read microchips.

Keep in mind that the Rottweiler's reputation for viciousness may discourage some people from attempting to help a lost pet. So in addition to providing your dog with at least two forms of identification, always go to extremes to prevent your Rottweiler from running away.

PET INSURANCE

Acting in the best interests of your dog includes providing him with health care, but what if you can't afford the veterinary bills? It can be challenging enough to pay for routine health examinations, but it can be financially devastating to face the costs associated with a major health condition or a serious injury.

Pet insurance operates in much the same way as health insurance for people. The pet owner pays an annual premium, the size of which depends on the insurance carrier, the level of coverage, the age of the pet, and other factors. The scope of coverage depends on the individual insurance company and the policy. Some policies provide coverage for routine veterinary care, like annual physical exams, while others cover only major medical expenses. Most pet insurance policies have a deductible, which means that the insurance carrier begins paying claims only after the pet owner has spent a certain amount of money out of pocket. Most plans also include co-payments for each visit to the veterinarian.

Is pet insurance worth the expense? Bear in mind that veterinary services have expanded rapidly in the last decade. Many of the same diagnostic and treatment options that are available to humans—such as MRIs, CT scans, and chemotherapy—are available to pets. This is great news for your dog's health, but it can be bad news for your wallet. Buying an insurance policy for your Rottweiler may make sense. If you are interested in pursuing this option, evaluate insurers and policies carefully. Be sure to check out the exclusions. Many policies won't cover hereditary problems or preexisting conditions.

In lieu of purchasing pet insurance, you might consider regularly putting aside a sum of money to cover future veterinary expenses. The best policy is to be prepared.

CANINE POPULATION CONTROL

Pet overpopulation is a pervasive problem in the United States and elsewhere. The Humane Society of the United States (HSUS) estimates that 3 million to 4 million cats and dogs are euthanized every year because there aren't enough homes for them. Rottweilers are popular dogs, so it may be hard to imagine that there is an abundance of homeless Rottweilers. However, that is the case. Responsible pet owners avoid contributing to the overpopulation problem by neutering or spaying their pets to prevent unwanted puppies.

Spayed or neutered Rottweilers are ineligible for certain dog shows, but unless you plan to show or breed your dog, there really aren't any good reasons not to have your Rottweiler surgically sterilized. Conversely, there are many reasons to have your dog neutered or spayed. Sterilization can make dogs better pets, by helping to eliminate sex-related behaviors that cause problems for dogs and their owners. In the case of male dogs, neutering helps subdue the urge to roam in search of mates. It also reduces the likelihood a dog will urinate on objects in or around the home to "mark" his territory. Neutering can also help lessen a male's aggressive tendencies—an important consideration with a dog like a Rottweiler.

Females that haven't been spayed go into a messy heat cycle twice per

FAST FACT

If you can't afford the fees charged by some vets for spaying or neutering, investigate a low-cost spay/neuter clinic. There you might pay as little as $50 for the surgery.

year and can easily produce unwanted litters. Repeated pregnancies take a toll on a female dog's health. Plus, a spayed female can't contract certain serious and potentially life-threatening conditions, such as pyometra (an infected uterus) or certain kinds of cancers.

Pet overpopulation is such a problem that several U.S. cities have actually considered making these surgeries mandatory for all pet dogs and cats. The reason for this is because the overpopulation issue isn't just a problem for the animals. It costs money and resources to deal with collecting, housing, and feeding unwanted animals, and finding new homes or euthanizing them. This problem can be a burden on the entire community.

LEGAL ISSUES

Some laws related to pet ownership have been on the books for a long time. Dog license ordinances, rabies laws, leash laws, liability laws, and nuisance laws are all designed for the welfare of the entire community. When responsible pet owners abide by these laws, everyone is safer and happier.

KNOW THE TRUTH

Don't believe these commonly held myths about the effects of sterilization surgery on your canine companion:

Myth: Neutering or spaying will change your dog's personality.
Fact: Sterilization surgery does not affect boldness, prey drive, energy level, or other personality traits. However, it does diminish or reduce unwanted behaviors associated with sexual drive.

Myth: Female dogs should have at least one litter before they are spayed.
Fact: A female dog does not benefit physically or temperamentally by having a litter. A female that is spayed prior to having a litter has a reduced chance of suffering certain health conditions, such as mammary tumors.

Myth: Dogs tend to become obese after sterilization surgery.
Fact: Neutering and spaying will not cause your dog to gain weight. Although it's true that sterilized dogs do not expend as much energy in search of mates, the only thing that really causes canine obesity is a combination of too many calories and not enough exercise.

LICENSING: Licensing is a tool used by communities to keep track of their pet populations. It provides a way to enforce household pet limits and to make sure that dogs in the community have had their rabies vaccinations. It also helps the local animal control official to identify dogs that have been found roaming the neighborhood.

Fines can be imposed on owners whose dogs are found to be unlicensed, so you'll want to apply for a license as soon as you can. Most communities expect their residents to obtain a license within a certain time period, such as within six months of acquiring a new dog. Proof that a dog has received its rabies vaccination may be required before a municipality will issue a license. For your community's licensing requirements, contact your local government or animal control office.

FAST FACT

Don't let financial hardship prevent you from providing necessary health care for your dog. A number of charities have been established to help elderly, low-income, or disadvantaged pet owners with veterinary expenses. Ask your veterinarian or local animal shelter if such a program exists in your area.

RABIES SHOTS: All states require dogs to be vaccinated against rabies, a neurological disease that causes horrific symptoms like delirium and erratic or vicious behavior. Rabies is a fatal disease that leads to a slow and painful death. It can be transmitted to humans, so for your own safety it's a good idea to protect your pet against this nasty virus.

There are different types of rabies vaccines. Some require annual booster shots, while others require boosters every three years. Your veterinarian will tell you which type of vaccine is required by your particular state. Most states now require the three-year vaccine.

LEASH LAWS: Public safety could not be assured without laws requiring dog owners to keep their pets under control. Many communities have enacted "leash laws," which are ordinances

FAST FACT

Most municipalities have restrictions on the number of dogs that can be kept in a household. If you plan on owning more than one dog, check with your municipality to find out how many dogs you are allowed to own.

that require dogs to be kept on leashes within the community limits. Responsible pet owners realize that keeping their dogs leashed is not just a way to prevent their dogs from causing mayhem to people and property; it also keeps their dogs safe.

No matter how well trained your Rottweiler is, keep him on a leash whenever you are out and about, and keep your dog under control at all other times. If you have a fenced yard for your outdoor-loving dog, make sure the fence is tall enough to keep him from jumping over it. Check the fence line occasionally to be sure he hasn't been trying to tunnel under it to freedom, and keep the fence and gate latches in good repair.

If you do not have a fence, it is important to never allow your Rottweiler off his leash in the yard until he is reliably trained to come when called. Even then, you should never leave your dog in an unfenced yard unattended. You need to take every possible precaution to prevent your Rottweiler from running at large. Even if your dog has friendly intentions, people have been conditioned to fear Rottweilers, and your neighbors may not appreciate your dog's efforts to say "hi."

LIABILITY ISSUES: In addition to leash laws, most communities have

A responsible pet owner cleans up after her pet when out in public.

liability laws that make a pet owner responsible for everything his or her dog does. If your Rottweiler injures someone or damages property, you are liable for that damage, even if it was accidental.

There are three very important things you can do to protect yourself from liability losses—take precautions, purchase liability insurance, and train your dog. Be prepared to

FAST FACT

Training is an integral component of responsible dog ownership. People don't appreciate dogs that jump all over them, knock their children down, bark or howl incessantly, or destroy their property. When you teach your dog not to do these things at home, your dog will display good manners in public as well.

provide supervision whenever your dog interacts with children. Make sure you have a homeowners or renters insurance policy in force to provide liability coverage both on and off your home premises. And invest as much training time into your dog as possible. A Rottweiler that is taught to respect humans, to come when called, and to have good manners is not apt to be a liability risk.

NUISANCE LAWS: Some laws exist to help dogs and humans live harmoniously together. This isn't an easy task, considering that dogs often engage in behaviors that humans find annoying. Incessant barking is a particularly nerve-wracking canine habit that can shatter the peace of a quiet neighborhood and deprive your neighbors of a good night's sleep.

This type of canine disturbance usually falls under a community's general nuisance law. Although Rottweilers are not known to be fanatical about barking, there is one situation, above all others, that tends to create a barker out of just about any dog—prolonged outdoor confinement. A dog left tied outside, kept in an outdoor kennel, or left unattended in a fenced yard is prone to become a nuisance barker out of boredom or loneliness. The solution is simple: don't leave your dog unattended outside for long periods of time.

Depending on how close you live to others, indoor barking can be just as disturbing to the general peace. If you manage your Rottweiler's barking properly from the beginning, it will help prevent your dog from getting into bad barking habits. This is done by praising your dog when he alerts you to appropriate situations (as a good canine guardian should), and rewarding him when he quiets down at your command. If your dog barks inappropriately, respond immediately to his alert. Using a firm voice, tell him "be quiet" or "no barking." If he responds to this command and stays quiet for about ten seconds, praise him and give him a treat or a favorite toy. Your Rottweiler will soon learn that his barking serves a very important purpose and that it's not appropriate to "cry wolf."

BE A GOOD NEIGHBOR

Abiding by the law is a great way to demonstrate that you are a responsible pet owner, but it's not enough. There are many "unwritten" laws that apply to pet ownership, most of which fall under the classification of courtesy. When you are courteous to others, you respect their feelings. You respect their space. And you respect their property.

Some people may not be very fond of dogs. Some people are fearful of them. And some people are allergic to them. You can avoid negative reactions from people by first asking them how they feel about your dog before introducing them to your pet. This is especially important for Rottweiler owners, as such a powerful dog understandably intimidates some people.

You will maintain the best of neighborly relations by not allowing your Rottweiler to trample your neighbors' flowerbed or dig up their newly planted garden, and you should take responsibility for the damage if he does. But the biggest pet peeve of neighbors, perhaps, is the "presents" that other people's dogs tend to leave on their lawns. It is absolutely imperative that you clean up after your dog while on walks and prevent your dog from

relieving himself on a neighbor's property or in a public area. Cleaning up after your pet is, after all, a part of caring for your dog that doesn't apply only to the messes he makes in his own yard.

≈≈≈≈

Responsible pet ownership is a concept loaded with positive fallout for people, dogs, and society in general. In the Rottweiler's case, it does even more than that. If irresponsible owners and breeders are mostly to blame for the negative image Rottweilers now endure, imagine the effect responsible pet owners can have on the reputation of this fine breed. You can enjoy a special sense of pride when you hear people comment, "Your dog has completely changed my mind about Rottweilers. What a great dog!"

CHAPTER FOUR

The Best Possible Beginning

Few things in life are as exciting as getting a new dog. Ideally, your new canine companion will adjust quickly to his new surroundings and get along well with everyone in the family, including other pets. This is certainly possible, but careful planning and preparation are required.

Avoid problems by assembling supplies for your Rottweiler and dog-proofing your home in advance.

SUPPLIES

Before you bring a dog home, be careful to purchase the supplies you'll need to care for him. Some of

Before choosing a Rottweiler, consider your family, lifestyle, and the size of your home.

these items may last your Rottweiler for his lifetime, so you want to be sure that they're right for your dog.

Food and water bowls come in a great variety of sizes and designs, but you should be more concerned with serviceability than style. It's better to avoid ceramic bowls, which can break, or plastic dishes, which harbor bacteria and are prone to damage from chewing. Stainless steel bowls are generally the most practical choice. They go with just about any type of décor, and they are dishwasher safe and easy to keep clean.

Collars and leashes can be picked to personalize your pup according to your taste. You will have to constantly check your growing puppy's collar to make sure it fits properly, and replace it when it has been outgrown. Both nylon and leather collars are exceptionally durable and make excellent ID tag holders. Choke chains and

pinch collars should not be worn as everyday neckwear. These collars are training aids, and should be removed when a dog is not in training.

You'll also need to assemble a grooming kit to care for your Rottweiler's coat, nails, teeth, and ears. A rubber curry brush or grooming mitt and a soft-bristled brush will take care of your Rottweiler's easy-to-care-for fur. A large pet nail clipper will tend to his pedicures, a canine dental kit will provide everything you need for his teeth, and some cotton balls and ear cleansing solution can help keep his ears clean. Although your Rottweiler should rarely require a bath, you'll want to stock up on bathing supplies in case your pet rolls in stinky stuff—which dogs are known to do occasionally.

Purchase a dog bed and other supplies before bringing your Rottweiler puppy home.

One of the most expensive items you may have to consider purchasing is a crate. Crates are marvelous inventions that have many great uses for pet owners. They can provide temporary confinement for your dog. They can provide a safe way to transport your pet. They can provide a safe place for your dog to rest or sleep, especially when he's a puppy. But when it comes to Rottweilers, crates have one large drawback—a crate big enough for a full-grown Rottweiler will take up an enormous amount of space in your home.

If a Rottweiler-sized crate (48 to 54 inches / 122 to 137 cm) is an eyesore in your living room and an imposing obstacle in your bedroom, you might want to consider purchasing door gates, so your pet can be confined in a room with an easy-to-clean tile floor. Door gates come in a large assortment of styles and sizes. A collapsible wire crate is another option. It can provide a source of confinement when you need it, but can be moved out of the way and stored when not in use. Eventually, though, you'll probably want to trade the crate for a more manageable dog bed. Rottweilers do not make the best bed partners or couch companions because of their size, so be prepared to purchase two beds: one for your buddy's sleeping quarters and

A Rottweiler's chew toys must be sturdy and durable. These powerful dogs can easily destroy cheap plastic toys, and there is a danger that splinters from a broken toy can injure your pet. Often, the packaging will indicate whether a toy is appropriate for strong, aggressive chewers like Rottweilers.

another for his living area. Your dog deserves a soft place to sleep at night, as well as a comfortable spot to recline during the day.

Finally, don't forget to give your new friend a few toys to play with. Part of the fun of getting a new dog is finding out what your dog likes: some Rottweilers are fetchers, some are tuggers, some love toys that squeak, and some are fanatical about chew toys. Always observe your dog closely when you give him something new. All dog toys are not safe for all dogs. If your Rottweiler tends to chew up or consume certain types of toys, you may have to look for something more heavy-duty. Invest in a small variety of toys to begin with, to learn which types of toys your dog likes and plays with safely.

DOG PROOFING YOUR HOME

Safety doesn't just apply to new toys. Your new pup won't know household rules at first. He will be curious about his new environment, and will probably explore it fearlessly. The best way to keep your puppy safe is to restrict him to certain areas of your home and make these places safe by "dog proofing" them.

Your dog's safe zone must be checked thoroughly for hazards. Get down on the floor and look at things from your dog's perspective. Electrical cords should be covered or raised. Toxic houseplants should be placed out of reach. Small objects that your dog could choke on should be removed. Since it's almost impossible to make a human environment 100 percent safe for a canine, you'll still have to observe your new pet closely to see what types of items attract him and teach him from the very beginning which items are not to be touched.

If you don't particularly appreciate teeth marks on your possessions, keep shoes, clothes, and children's toys off the floor until your dog learns to play with his own things. You can help your dog learn the difference between "your stuff" and "his stuff" by giving him a toy box to hold his things. A cardboard box works just fine. Your dog will appreciate knowing where to find his toys when he wants them, and these items will have his scent on them so he'll know they're his.

LIVING ARRANGEMENTS

Your Rottweiler has to adjust to a new home and a new family. You, too, will have some adjustments to make. Getting a new Rottweiler means there will be another body in your home. This body may be small to begin with, but it will grow to become quite large. Where is your dog going to fit? Where is he going to eat? Where is he going to sleep? Where is he going to be kept when you can't be there to supervise? Where is he going to go to the bathroom? All of these things are best determined in advance.

EATING ARRANGEMENTS: When choosing a place for your new pup to dine, you'll want a spot that is easy to keep clean. The kitchen is generally the most practical choice, as it usually has an easy-to-clean floor as well as a water source. There is probably a convenient cabinet where his food can be stored, also. However, keep your new dog's needs in mind, too. Your Rottweiler should not have to tolerate people stepping on him or bumping into him when he's trying to eat. He shouldn't have to put up with children harassing him during mealtime, or compete with other pets for food. So find a spot where your dog can eat in peace. If you have other pets, you may need to feed your animals in separate rooms or in their crates to prevent fights over food.

SLEEPING ARRANGEMENTS: Until your dog is housetrained and can be trusted throughout the house, you'll want to bed down your Rottweiler where you can keep an eye on him. For a puppy, this means crating him at night to prevent accidents. Dogs will try not to soil their sleeping areas. However, you may need to get up and let your dog out every four hours or so, at least until he's six months old and his bladder is large enough to last through the night.

As your Rottweiler matures, he will let you know his sleeping preferences—beside your bed, in the bedroom of a favorite child, or perhaps outside a bedroom door, where he can do a proper job of guarding the family.

OFF-LIMITS AREAS: There may be some rooms in your home that will have to be off limits until your dog learns household rules. There may also be some areas, either indoors or outdoors, that should be permanently off-limits to your new canine housemate. A young, rambunctious Rottweiler can be like a bull in a china shop if he gets rowdy in the house, so you'll probably want to keep him out of the computer room, hobby room, or anyplace else where dangerous materials or delicate possessions are kept.

Outdoors, you'll want to teach your new canine pupil to stay out of the flower garden and not to explore the lumber pile where a hidden nail might pierce his paw. Garages and tool sheds often contain many dangers, such as hazardous fuels and solvents or sharp tools. Identify such areas before you bring your new friend home, so you can enforce rules from the start.

POTTY AREA: Before bringing a dog home, choose an outdoor spot where he can go to the bathroom. Having a designated potty area has several advantages. The most significant is that it helps when housetraining your dog. The smell of a previously soiled area stimulates a dog to "go," so once you get your dog in the habit of using a particular spot, it's easier to teach him when and where he's supposed to go. A designated potty place also makes for easier yard cleanup. Who wants to search the whole yard for dog waste? So choose a convenient area for this purpose and use it consistently after your pup comes home.

HOUSEHOLD RULES AND RESPONSIBILITIES

It's important to establish rules for your Rottweiler, but these rules will mean absolutely nothing if they are not enforced consistently. This means there also have to be rules for household members, especially children. Everyone in the family must know that it's not appropriate to feed your dog from the table, disturb him when he's eating, or allow him to roam through off-limits areas. If you don't clearly communicate the rules to everyone in the family, your effort at training the dog can be inadvertently sabotaged by a family member who is not following the program.

It is a good idea to get everyone in the family involved with your new dog's care. Children who do not participate in the care of a family pet do not reap the full benefits of the pet ownership experience. Caring for a pet dog is more than a way to teach children responsibility; it allows children to develop a special relationship with their canine pal. A Rottweiler tends to bond strongly to the people who care for him.

Pet care chores obviously need to be age-appropriate, but there are many tasks from which to choose. Feeding, watering, walking, grooming, yard cleanup, training (with adult guidance), and even playing (exercise) all offer opportunities for children to be important parts of their dog's life.

WHAT TO EXPECT THE FIRST FEW NIGHTS

Adjusting to a completely new environment and routine is not easy. Be patient with your new Rottweiler. It's not unusual for a puppy to cry for its mother and littermates during the first few nights. But there are a few things you can do to make this time easier for both you and your lonely pup. First, make sure your puppy has had a good play session in the evening so he'll be tired at bedtime. Don't over-do the exercise, though. If your pup becomes overstimulated, it may take a long time for him to settle down. Give your puppy a light snack shortly before bed—eating can make a dog feel a little drowsy. Finally, make sure your puppy has a potty break before tucking him in at night.

Make sure your pup is as comfortable as possible with soft bedding. Give your little guy a hot water bottle wrapped in a towel to cuddle with. The warmth will simulate the warm bodies of the canine family he misses. If you've purchased your puppy from

RULES FOR CHILDREN

The following are some good rules to discuss with children:

- Don't feed the dog from the table.
- Don't disturb the dog while he's eating.
- Don't allow the puppy to nip at your hands and feet.
- Don't allow the dog to jump on you.
- Put your toys away so the dog won't chew them.
- Encourage the dog to play with his own toys.
- Praise the dog when he behaves well.

a breeder, she may give you a piece of blanket or shirt that has his mother's scent on it. That may also help comfort your pet when it's bedtime. Your puppy will feel most secure if he knows you are nearby, so you may want to move his crate into your bedroom for the first few nights.

Once your pup has settled into his crate for the night, it's important to leave him there. It takes an awful lot of willpower to ignore a puppy's cries, but the truth is that your puppy will adjust much faster if you establish your nighttime routine from the very beginning. If you keep getting up to fuss over him, it will take longer to get your puppy to go to sleep and you'll prolong your pup's adjustment period. This will cost you more sleep in the long run. With a regular routine, most puppies will stop fussing after two or three nights.

INTRODUCING OTHER PETS

How you introduce your Rottweiler to your other pets will affect the relationship those animals will develop. Sometimes pets hit it off from the very first day and become fast friends. Other times, it takes pets a while before they decide they like each other. On occasion, however, pets never become friends—and they may or may not even learn to tolerate each other.

You can imagine a resident cat will not welcome a boisterous Rottweiler pup with open paws. This doesn't mean they can't learn to get along. But until your puppy matures and has a better idea of how to interact with a sensitive feline, you'll need to provide a safe escape for your cat. Here's a situation where door gates are invaluable. A standard-sized gate will contain a puppy, but a cat can jump over the gate and escape if she feels harassed. As long as your cat has a place to which she can safely retreat, you can allow your pets to get to know each other on their own terms and in their own time.

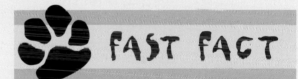

FAST FACT

Care must be taken when attempting to integrate different animal species within the same home, especially if you are combining a predator species, like a dog, with a prey species, like a rabbit. A puppy that is raised with prey animals is more likely to learn to get along with them. But if your Rottweiler continually harasses your prey-species pets, it is best to find a new home for one or the other. It is not fair to require a sensitive prey animal to tolerate the stress and anxiety associated with the constant harassment from a predator.

When it comes to introducing dogs to each other, things usually go a little smoother. Dogs are "pack" animals, and as such, they naturally like the company of other canines. If you introduce your Rottweiler to a resident dog, it is best to do it on neutral territory, away from home, with both dogs on leashes. Some dogs hit if off marvelously from their first encounter. If both dogs seem polite to each other, take them for a walk together. This is a great way to help canines "break the ice" and feel more comfortable with each other before asking them to share living space. Gradually allow the dogs to have more contact. When you see one dog offer the other a play-bow gesture, you'll know they've become friends.

COGNITIVE AND SOCIAL DEVELOPMENT

Dogs go through developmental stages until they reach adulthood, just as humans do. Between 6 and 12 weeks of age, puppies go through a stage in which they need to be exposed to many new people and animals. Socialization helps dogs learn how to trust people, how to get along with other animals, and how to adapt to new situations. During this time, puppies go through a "fear-imprint period." If

they have a painful or traumatic experience with a certain stimulus, they are likely to develop a deep-rooted, generalized fear. For example, a puppy that has been hurt by a child during the fear-imprint period can easily become terrified of all children throughout his life.

Proper socialization is especially important for Rottweilers, which are purposely bred to have a protective nature. Without plenty of socialization, a Rottweiler may become overly reactive to unknown people or animals. You can help your Rottweiler to develop healthy social perspectives by taking him to parks, pet stores, training classes, or anyplace else where he can get a taste of the outside world. Make sure to keep these experiences very positive for your impressionable pup, and enjoy them as opportunities to show off your handsome new companion.

As your puppy matures, he'll develop more independence, and maybe a bit of belligerence, too. Between six months and two years of age, dogs go through a challenging developmental period that some people refer to as the "teenage years." This stage can be particularly noticeable with the independent-minded Rottweiler. Dogs of this age need to test limits to determine where they fit within the social hierarchy. They often have an insatiable urge to explore and learn about the world around them, and they haven't yet had a chance to develop much self-control. In other words, they don't always listen very well.

This is a challenging but very crucial developmental period that demands firm, consistent handling for your Rottweiler. It's also an excellent time to focus on training. Dogs in this age group have gained a greater attention span and tend to retain things easier than they did as puppies. If you make it clear to your Rottweiler what you expect of him at this age, it will help you establish a mutually respectful relationship that will last throughout your dog's life. This is, perhaps, the best beginning you could possibly provide for your canine friend.

CANINE DEVELOPMENT MILESTONES

Up to 8 weeks: A puppy learns canine communication signals and other social skills from his mother and littermates. This is why it is important not to remove a puppy from his mother until he is at least 8 weeks old.

8 to 12 weeks: A puppy has a natural desire to stay close to his human "surrogate parent." He also goes through a fear development stage where he may show a fear of unfamiliar things or situations. It is important to expose the puppy to plenty of positive opportunities for socialization during this period.

12 weeks to 6 months: A puppy begins to develop some independence. He may still show some apprehension about unfamiliar people or situations.

Exposure to many different experiences is still very important.

6 months to 2 years: During a dog's "teenage years," he will be very curious about the outside world and test his limits to see where he fits within the social hierarchy. Dogs learn rapidly at this age. Rottweilers have puppy-sized energy in an adult-sized body during this period.

Over 2 years: The wild behaviors of the teenage years begin to subside. A Rottweiler becomes more physically and mentally mature. Ability to concentrate and focus becomes even stronger, making this a great time to pursue canine sports or other endeavors that involve advanced training.

CHAPTER FIVE

Nutrition, Exercise, Grooming, and Training

Rottweilers are high-maintenance pets, and when you choose to own one be prepared for a lot of responsibility. The most labor-intensive activities are feeding, exercising, grooming, and training. Although these activities require time and energy, they offer many benefits as well. Studies have shown that people who own pets live longer and recuperate from illnesses more quickly than people who don't. Pets help give people purposeful lives, they are a good source of exercise, and, of course, they provide an abundance of healing love. So just remember that

Your Rottweiler will need at least two 20-minute exercise periods each day.

fulfilling your Rottweiler's care requirements is as good for you as it is for your dog.

APPROPRIATE NUTRITION FOR YOUR ROTTWEILER

During their first eight weeks of life, puppies need the high fat content and immunity-boosting nutrition of their mother's milk. Although moist canned foods may be introduced when a dog is four to five weeks old, and dry foods can be introduced at six weeks of age, puppies still require their mother's milk for proper development. Reputable breeders won't let you take a new puppy home until he is at least eight weeks of age and has been weaned from his mother.

Before bringing a Rottweiler puppy home, ask the breeder about the type and brand of food she used to wean your puppy. Feeding your dog the same type of food for at least a couple of weeks will help his digestive system. Your breeder may even give you a

small amount of food to take home with your dog. Eventually, though, you may want to switch to another brand of dog food. When you're ready to do this, there are a few things to keep in mind.

PUPPIES NEED PUPPY FOOD: Your Rottweiler puppy will need a commercial dog food formulated especially for puppies. This type of food has the higher calorie content necessary to fuel your dog's rapid physical growth during this stage of life. When your dog approaches his mature height, at around ten to twelve months of age, he'll be ready for an adult formula food.

CHANGE YOUR PUPPY'S DIET GRADUALLY: A sudden change in diet is stressful to your dog's digestive system

To prevent bloat, a potentially deadly condition caused by an accumulation of gas and air in a large dog's stomach, feed your Rottweiler two smaller meals rather than one large meal each day. It also helps to avoid exercising your Rottweiler one hour before and two hours after feeding.

and will undoubtedly cause diarrhea. This does not only result in dreadful messes in the house; it can also slow the process of housetraining your pup. Instead, mix a little of the new food into a larger portion of the old food. Over a two-week period, gradually increase the proportion of new food to old, until your dog is eating only the new food.

CHOOSE A QUALITY PUPPY FOOD: You can't tell the quality of a commercially prepared dog food by looking at it. Foods that are made to look more attractive with cute shapes and appealing colors may actually contain inferior ingredients and undesirable additives. Price, too, is not always an accurate determinant of quality. Take the time to read the label and find out what you are putting into your dog.

Quality dog foods use a meat product (not "by-product") as a main source of protein, and this should be listed as the first item on the ingredient list. Quality foods use few grain products, and they also use natural forms of preservatives, such as Vitamins E and C (sometimes listed as "mixed tocopherols"). They also include a good source of omega-3 and omega-6 fatty acids, such as flaxseed oil or fish oil, to keep your dog's skin and coat in top condition.

A dog food that meets these requirements will have a dramatic

PLAYING WITH FOOD

Obviously, you can't participate in activities with your Rottweiler all the time. One way to keep your Rottweiler occupied, and out of trouble, when you're away is to stuff a toy with food.

You can use any type of heavy-duty rubber dog toy that has a cavity suitable for stuffing, and fill it almost full (leave about half an inch open) with your dog's kibble. Fill the remaining space with soft food like canned dog food, peanut butter, liver sausage, or vanilla yogurt. Freeze the toy overnight so the soft food becomes hard, then give it to your dog.

Your dog will figure out how to get the frozen "plug" out of the toy so the kibble falls out. After this, you can make things a little more challenging by alternating layers of kibble and soft food when you stuff the toy.

Always remember to count such a treat as part of your dog's daily food intake, so that he doesn't gain weight.

effect on the health and appearance of your dog. It can keep your Rottweiler's coat lustrously black and give him the energy and vitality to enjoy life. It can add a year or more to his lifespan, and save you plenty in veterinary expenses over the years.

NUTRITION FOR YOUR ADULT ROTTWEILER

Choosing a quality dog food doesn't just apply to puppies. When your dog is ready to transition to an adult formula food, you'll have to evaluate your choices all over again. As always, it's a good idea to change your dog's diet gradually at this stage. You'll also have to become more observant of your dog's weight, as your dog will no longer be able to benefit from a puppy's ability to "grow into" an extra pound or two.

Rottweilers possess a lot of natural bulk, so it's easy for excess weight to escape your attention until your Rottweiler becomes obviously barrel-shaped. You can help your Rottweiler avoid gaining unwanted weight by engaging in the following good feeding practices:

- Use a cup or scoop to measure your dog's food.
- Monitor your dog's weight and adjust the amount you feed him accordingly.
- Feed your dog regularly twice per day.
- Remove uneaten food after 20 minutes—don't leave food out for your dog to nibble on during the day.
- Limit your dog's consumption of "people food," treats, and consumable chew products.

ALTERNATIVE DIETS

Commercially prepared diets for dogs have come a long way in the last couple decades. Quality has improved, and choices have multiplied. Still, there is a growing interest in alternative diets.

Some dog owners and experts recommend raw foods as the natural foundation for the canine diet. The popular Bones and Raw Food (BARF) diet is now available in the form of commercially packaged frozen patties. You simply thaw them out before feeding them to your dog.

Although some owners prefer to prepare their own raw food meals for their dogs, the advantage of purchasing commercially packaged raw food is that all the necessary vitamins and supplements have already been added. Your dog's diet will be healthy and balanced.

Home-cooked diets have also gained many fans among dog lovers. Basically, home-cooked dog food consists of "people food" such as meat, eggs, cottage cheese, and vegetables. Ingredients must be assembled in the right proportions, and vitamins and supplements must be added in order for the diet to be nutritionally complete.

Alternative diets may offer the opportunity to provide the healthiest food possible for your dog. But if you don't prepare the food properly, your dog may have a nutritionally inadequate diet. Do plenty of research on alternative diets before putting your Rottweiler on one.

If you'd like to give your Rottweiler a chance to run off-leash in an open field where other people might be present, consider outfitting him with a muzzle for safety. A wire basket muzzle, like the one pictured above, has certain advantages. It allows your Rottweiler to pant freely and to drink when needed.

EXERCISE

A good quality dog food will provide your dog with a good source of energy, but how will your Rottweiler expend that energy? Dogs that don't receive enough exercise can become frustrated and destructive. Adequate exercise is especially important for large dogs. If a Rottweiler doesn't get the chance to work his muscles, imagine how much trouble he could get into!

A game of fetch, playtime with another dog, or any other activity that gets your dog running is a great way to give your Rottweiler's cardiovascular system a workout and let him burn off excess energy. Try to spend at least 40 minutes per day playing with your dog or engaging in one of the many appropriate canine sports or activities. Rottweilers can make excellent jogging, bicycling, or hiking partners. Exercise will keep your dog healthy while providing a source of fun and entertainment for both of you.

GROOMING YOUR ROTTWEILER

Although Rottweilers need plenty of exercise time, they require much less attention in the grooming department. However, some grooming is important, and not just to make your dog look his best. Regular brushing and grooming will significantly reduce the amount of hair shed in your house. It also desensitizes your dog to being handled and contributes to his overall health.

COAT CARE: Your Rottweiler's coat will require no more than a light brushing once a week. A good massage with a rubber curry brush or mitt will stimulate the skin and bring dead hair and dandruff to the coat's surface. This is a part of grooming that your dog will thoroughly enjoy. Brush in circular motions over the whole body and pay particular attention to those areas your dog obviously likes, like the rump and neck.

After this is done, brush your dog's coat with a soft-bristled brush, following the direction in which the hairs grow. For a polishing touch, you can wipe him down with a damp cloth or chamois skin to distribute the coat's natural oils. This will give your Rottweiler's black coat an incredible shine.

BATHING: Fortunately, a Rottweiler's short coat doesn't require bathing very often, but you should be prepared to bathe your dog at least a few times per year. Attempting to bathe a full-grown Rottweiler may seem intimidating, but having the proper supplies on hand before you start will make the task easier. Your bathtub can make a perfect dog wash if you equip it with a large rubber

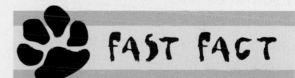

FAST FACT

Following are the supplies that you'll need to properly groom your Rottweiler:
- Rubber curry brush or mitt
- Soft-bristled bush
- Large nail clipper
- Toothbrush and paste
- Dog Shampoo
- Cotton balls (to keep ears dry)
- Towels
- Rubber mat
- Spray nozzle

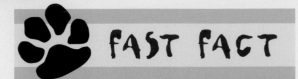

FAST FACT

Always use dog shampoos when bathing your Rottweiler. Human shampoos are too harsh for pets.

mat, so your dog won't slip in the tub, and a spray nozzle. Many pet supply stores and catalogs sell spray nozzles that can be plugged into a shower pipe and removed when they are not needed. You'll need an apron or smock, because it's almost impossible to wash a dog this size without getting a little wet. You'll also want to bring cotton balls, dog shampoo, a few treats, and towels for drying.

Start by placing your dog in the unfilled tub, and placing cotton balls in his ears so that water doesn't get into his ear canals. Wet down his coat with lukewarm water, using the shower hose or a plastic pitcher. Try not to get your Rottweiler's head wet—once a dog's head gets wet, he will want to shake off the water. Dilute a quarter-cup of the dog shampoo in about a gallon of warm water; this will make the soap easier to work into and rinse out of your Rottweiler's coat. Apply the diluted shampoo and lather it through the coat, starting at the neck and working toward the tail. Lather your dog's

head last, being very careful not to get shampoo or water in your Rottweiler's eyes, ears, or nose. You can use a soft cloth and warm water to gently wash his face.

When you're done, rinse the soap out of his coat, starting with the head and working toward his tail. Be sure to thoroughly rinse out all the shampoo. Any residue that remains in his coat will attract dirt, make his coat feel sticky, and cause dry, itchy skin. Once the coat has been rinsed clean, you can hand-dry your Rottweiler using a soft, fluffy towel.

Throughout the bathing process, praise and encourage your dog to relax him, and dole out treats periodically to reward good behavior in the tub. Try to keep the experience as positive as possible for him. You don't want bath time to become a battle, because it's no fun, and usually fruitless, to battle with a Rottweiler. Brush or comb your dog's hair immediately after bathing.

EAR CARE: Ear care is especially important for your Rottweiler because floppy-eared dogs do not always get enough air circulation under the ears to keep their ear canals dry. The moisture that gets trapped there provides a fertile breeding ground for bacteria, which causes ear infections.

You can help prevent ear infections in your Rottweiler by putting cotton balls in his ears prior to a bath to keep the water out. In addition, clean your dog's ears regularly with a canine ear cleaner that contains a drying agent like alcohol. You can find ear cleaners at most pet supply stores, or you can ask your veterinarian to recommend an appropriate product.

NAIL CARE: Your Rottweiler's nails will grow continuously, so you'll have to trim them about every three weeks. Clipping a dog's nails can be intimidating if you've never done this before. There is always a fear of clipping the nail too short and causing the dog to suffer pain and bleeding.

Thankfully, there are easy ways to avoid this.

A good practice is to clip a little bit of the nail at a time. You can tell you are getting close to the quick, which is the nail's blood supply, when you see a small black dot in the center of the clipped surface of the nail. This is an indication to stop clipping. It's always better to leave the nails a little too long than to cut them too short.

Begin by supporting your dog's paw and selecting a toe, then look for the quick—the blood vessels and nerves inside the nail. The quick will look like a line running through the center of the nail that doesn't quite reach the tip. On dark or black nails, the quick can be hard to see, but it

A good rule of thumb is, if you can hear a dog's nails clicking when he walks on a wood, linoleum, or tile floor, his nails are too long.

must be avoided. Trim off little bits at a time until you are sure of the quick's location. If you cut too deep, you'll nick the blood vessels, causing bleeding and pain. In that case, apply styptic powder, cornstarch, or a coagulant to stop the bleeding. Be sure to speak to your Rottweiler in a soothing voice throughout the procedure so that he is put at ease. When you're finished, give him a treat and lots of praise.

The top surface of a nail always grows faster than the bottom surface, which is why a dog's nails grow into a hooked shape. With practice, you can determine the excess growth of the nail simply by looking at the nail from the side to see the length of the hook.

If you are worried about tackling this task, there are other options. Battery-operated nail files are available that will allow you to grind your dog's nails down a little at a time. If all else fails, enlist the aid of your veterinarian or a professional

groomer. Regardless of who performs your dog's pedicures, you should make a point of handling your Rottweiler's feet and toes frequently so he will learn to tolerate this very necessary procedure.

DENTAL CARE: It may take some time for your dog to learn to tolerate having his mouth handled, too. Dogs enjoy having their teeth brushed about as much as they enjoy baths, but you can gain your Rottweiler's cooperation by being patient, taking it slow, and rewarding your dog for his good behavior.

Dental care is now recognized as a very necessary part of dog ownership. Wild canines clean their teeth naturally by chewing on the fibrous tissues of their prey. Domestic dogs, on the other hand, eat processed food that tends to collect on the teeth. It's no wonder most domestic dogs suffer from some degree of periodontal disease. Periodontal disease can lead to serious health problems, as infections from the mouth can travel to other parts of the body. But that's not the only reason to keep your dog's ivories clean. Regular dental care also helps to minimize a common canine problem—dog breath!

When your puppy is six months old, you should develop a biweekly

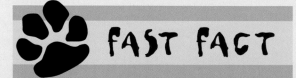

FAST FACT

When trimming your dog's nails, if you can't see the quick, clip slowly and carefully. It's better to leave his nails a little too long than to cut them too short.

brushing routine. Plaque will begin to develop on a puppy's permanent teeth at this age and should be removed periodically to avoid buildup. Brushing should be done with a specially formulated doggie toothpaste and toothbrush. These items can be purchased from a pet supply store or veterinarian's office. You should never use human toothpaste to brush a Rottweiler's teeth. Human toothpaste is harsh and may upset a dog's stomach. Always brush your dog's teeth gently using the amount of paste recommended on

the tube. Make as many vertical passes with the brush as you can, lifting your dog's lips whenever necessary to get the outer surface of each tooth.

You can supplement brushing with chew toys and other products that are specifically designed to remove tartar buildup. These toys can be purchased from pet supply stores and may be available through your veterinarian's office.

When you take your Rottweiler for his annual checkup, your vet will examine your pet's teeth and check for early signs of periodontal disease. If necessary, your vet can also scale and polish your Rottweiler's teeth.

You'll need to brush your Rottweiler's teeth at least twice a week to keep them clean and reduce the likelihood of gum disease.

TRAINING YOUR ROTTWEILER

While you are putting the effort into caring for your Rottweiler's physical needs, don't forget to take care of his intellectual needs. Dogs are not born knowing how to be good pets; they only know how to be dogs. Your Rottweiler has the potential to be an excellent companion, but he needs your help.

HOUSETRAINING

The most important requirement for a good house pet is for him to learn where it is appropriate to eliminate.

In order to get through the house-training process as quickly as possible with the least amount of accidents, there are three things to keep in mind: prevention, anticipation, and rewards.

Prevention consists of confining or supervising your Rottweiler at all times until he is reliably house-trained. It's difficult for your dog to have an accident if he never has the opportunity. A young puppy's confinement area may need to have an appropriate potty area with newspapers or puppy pads, especially if the puppy needs to be confined for several hours. When supervising your puppy outside of his confinement area, watch for the warning signs that he may need to go, like sniffing the ground, circling, or arching his back. Then, get him out to his designated outdoor potty area right away.

Anticipation means being proactive in getting your puppy to his potty area when he is most likely to need it. It's common for puppies to eliminate after eating, sleeping, or exercising. If you keep your puppy on a regular schedule for these activities, he'll soon develop a regular potty schedule as well. It is much easier for a puppy to learn to hold his waste if he can count on being let outside at the same times every day.

Housetraining takes a lot of effort from your furry friend. If you want to convince your puppy that it's worth his while, reward him with a special treat whenever he eliminates

A crate can be very useful when housetraining a Rottweiler puppy. Dogs do not like to urinate or defecate where they sleep, so they generally will not go to the bathroom in their crates.

in the right spot. This can help speed up the housetraining process considerably.

Regardless of how diligent you are about confining, supervising, anticipating and rewarding your puppy, some accidents are inevitable. If you catch your pup attempting to eliminate in the house, rush him outside to his potty area. Then, clean up any messes with a cleaning product designed to neutralize pet odors. Be kind to your puppy during this process. It's not fair to punish a puppy for a skill he obviously hasn't mastered yet. Rubbing your dog's nose in a puddle of his urine won't teach him not to go to the bathroom indoors. It will only teach him that you're mean and not to be trusted.

CRATE TRAINING

You can train your Rottweiler to accept crate confinement by introducing him to the crate gradually. Try to convince your dog to enter the crate willingly by putting toys or treats in or near the door of the crate. As his comfort level grows, you can put toys or treats further into the crate. When he begins to enter the crate on his own, you can add a command, like "kennel," so your dog will learn to enter the crate when you tell him to. Reward him when he responds to this command.

When you are not crate training, leave the crate accessible to your dog so he can explore it at his leisure. Make it as enticing and comfortable as possible by furnishing it with a comfortable bed and putting some favorite toys inside. Your dog might even start using the crate as a resting place without any prompting.

When your dog seems comfortable with the idea of spending time in his crate, you can begin to close the door and confine your dog for short periods of time. It will help to give your dog a chew toy or something to keep him busy. If your dog begins to fuss, wait until he's quiet before you let him out, as you do not

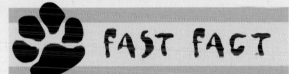

FAST FACT

How long should you crate your dog? A puppy should not be left in his crate for more than an hour for every month of its age. For instance, a two-month-old puppy can be crated for a maximum of two hours, a three-month-old puppy can be crated up to three hours, and so on. Always make sure your dog has had a potty break before crating, and never leave any dog in his crate for more than six hours. If you need to confine your dog for a longer period, he'll need a larger confinement area, such as a mud room with a door gate.

Even if you are perfectly capable of training a Rottweiler at home, participating in an obedience class is a great way to teach your dog to be reliable amongst the distractions of a public setting. Obedience classes can provide opportunities to socialize your dog, and the support of an expert training instructor is invaluable.

want to reward him for fussing. As your dog learns to tolerate short confined periods, you can gradually increase the length of confinement.

BASIC OBEDIENCE

Obedience training is so important for a strong dog like a Rottweiler that many breeders and Rottweiler rescue groups will not allow you to purchase or adopt a Rottweiler

unless you enroll in an obedience training class. An out-of-control Rottweiler is like a runaway tractor-trailer—large and scary. If you are not an experienced dog trainer, it's essential that you become educated before you acquire a Rottweiler.

Always evaluate a training class before enrolling in it to make sure the instructor uses positive training methods. Rottweilers do not respond well to heavy-handed training methods. However, you also have to be careful to choose an instructor who emphasizes canine leadership and doesn't rely entirely on food rewards to influence canine behavior. Fair, consistent, and firm handling is required if you want your Rottweiler to become a congenial companion.

Teaching your Rottweiler basic obedience skills—come, sit, down, and stay—will enable you to control your pet's movements. A dog that responds well to these commands is like an extension of his owner's mind and body. If you want to achieve that level of control, spend at least 10 minutes three times per week training your dog.

COME: The "come" command is the most important, and sometimes the most challenging, skill to teach a dog. Dogs live in a world of intriguing smells, sights, and other distractions. They are sometimes overpowered by curiosity or instincts, so it's no

wonder they find it difficult to come when called. But plenty of practice can help condition your dog to respond to the "come" command consistently.

To teach and reinforce this skill, carry treats around with you and call your dog frequently during the day from different rooms in your home. Call him only once each time and reward him when he responds. Once your dog is responding regularly inside the house, you can start to practice outside where there are more distractions. Always practice in a fenced area or with your dog on a long line to keep him safe. However,

Good training is imperative for Rottweilers because of their size and strength. These dogs must be trained to respond immediately to your commands.

Teaching a dog to sit will help him learn other skills, such as "down" and "stay."

keep his eyes on the treat, he should automatically back up into a sit. When he does, reward him immediately with a piece of the treat. If not, experiment with using the treat as a lure until you can manipulate your dog into a sitting position, then reward him. Repeat this exercise several times each day, using the "sit" command so your dog learns to associate it with the sit position.

DOWN: Once your dog has mastered the "sit" command, he's ready to learn "down." Start your dog in a seated position, then hold a treat close to the floor in front of him. Slowly draw the treat away from him. This will encourage your dog to stretch out for the treat. If his front end drops even a little bit, let him have a piece of the treat. If he tries to stand up, put him back into a sit and start over, being careful not to progress too quickly. By rewarding your dog for gradual progress, your dog will eventually stretch out until he achieves a full down. You can then start using the "down" command so he can associate it with the position.

don't use the line to force your dog to come if he doesn't respond, as that will teach him that obedience only applies while he's on a line. With constant practice in successively more distracting environments, your Rottweiler will learn to respond reliably.

SIT: The "sit" command can be taught by holding a treat just above your dog's head and moving it slowly toward his back. As your dog tries to

STAY: It is also easier to teach the "stay" command when your dog starts in a sitting position, as this is a comfortable position for a dog to maintain for a period of time. Stand in front of your sitting dog. Tell him to stay as you take a quick step backward, then immediately step forward again. If your dog maintains his seated position, reward him with part of a treat. When your dog masters this very short stay, gradually increase the distance you step away from your dog while also increasing the amount of time you expect your dog to maintain the position. If you progress slowly and reward your dog for correct responses, your dog will eventually learn to stay even when you're out of his sight.

WALKING ON A LEASH PROPERLY

Dogs must be trained not to tug or pull incessantly against the leash. This is particularly true of large dogs like Rottweilers. A full-grown

FOOD REWARD TIPS

Avoid processed meats, which contain undesirable additives. Also avoid dairy products, like cheese, which can cause digestive problems. Pieces of cooked and chopped beef, chicken, pork, or liver are highly motivating, healthier treat choices.

Limit the amount of treats you use for training sessions, and decrease your dog's dinner rations in proportion to the amount of treats he consumes so your dog doesn't gain unwanted weight.

Once your dog has learned a particular skill, you do not need to give him a treat every time he executes that command. Start phasing out the treats by rewarding your dog every other time he performs the skill, then every three times, and so on, until your dog behaves on command without the food incentive.

If your Rottweiler obviously knows obedience commands, but refuses to obey unless you have food to offer, he has become "food dependent." You'll need to work on your canine leadership skills to gain your Rottweiler's respect and strengthen his will to please.

Rottweiler can be downright deadly at the end of a leash if he has not been taught to walk properly. If your Rottweiler is a puller, you'll have to be very consistent in not allowing this behavior. When he pulls, stop and wait for your dog to slacken the leash before you continue. You can also turn around and start walking in the opposite direction, forcing him to come back to you. After a while, your dog should realize that pulling won't get him anywhere.

If your determined Rottweiler has a lot of difficulty with this lesson and is too powerful to control, don't be afraid to try training aids, like a pinch collar. It's best to use these

WHAT IS A CANINE LEADER?

A canine leader is:

Firm: Firm leaders aren't afraid to talk sternly to their dogs when necessary. Dogs are very sensitive to your tone of voice. A firm voice indicates confidence and control, and Rottweilers respect those who give them a sense of security through firm leadership.

Fair: Fair leaders recognize and reward good behavior. They have clear expectations and communicate them in ways a dog can understand. They never blame a dog for behaving like a dog, and they never ask a dog to do anything unsafe or beyond the dog's capabilities. Rottweilers trust those who treat them fairly.

Consistent: Good leaders are not wishy-washy; they have consistent expectations. A Rottweiler sees consistency as an indication of stability and

trustworthiness, two major components in earning a Rottweiler's trust and respect.

A canine leader is not:

Physically dominant: Physical force and violence, or even the threat of these things, are the signs of a tyrant, not a leader. Tyrants earn no one's respect, although they do tend to fuel insurgencies. You do not want to be on the receiving end of a Rottweiler's revolt!

Dictatorial: Dictators have to be in control at all times and don't care what anyone else thinks. But a good canine leader realizes that dogs are not robots. Pay attention to what your dog tries to tell you, try to understand the reasons for his disobedience, and gain his willing compliance through a strong bond, not force.

The "heel" command requires your Rottweiler to walk at your left side.

items under the guidance of an experienced dog trainer. You absolutely must be able to control your Rottweiler on a leash, so be persistent and make sure your dog gets the message that straining against the leash is not acceptable.

The "heel" command requires a dog to walk very close to his master's side. Although this is required to show good control and discipline in obedience competitions, it's not really necessary to make your dog maintain this position during everyday walks. If you want to teach your Rottweiler this command, at the start of your walk position the dog on your left side and instruct him to sit. Raise your left foot and begin walking. As soon as your foot leaves the ground, issue the command "heel" in a firm tone. If your dog tries to run ahead or lag behind, stop and issue the "heel" command again. When you stop, tell the dog to sit. If necessary, pull up on the leash very gently to coax him into a sitting position. When you begin walking again, command your Rottweiler to heel. If you repeat this exercise for a few minutes each day, several times per day, and offer encouragement, praise, and the occasional treat for motivation, your Rottweiler should learn how to walk on a leash in no time.

❧❧❧❧

Caring for and training your Rottweiler is not a thankless job; your effort will always be repaid. Your Rottweiler's gratitude will be obvious by his excitement at feeding time, his anticipation of play time, his pleasure in grooming, and his enthusiasm for training. People, too, will compliment you on your beautiful, well-behaved canine.

CHAPTER SIX

Health Issues Your Rottweiler May Face

Caring for the health of your Rottweiler is a big job that requires the assistance of a professional. You'll want to find a veterinarian you can trust, who is knowledgeable and competent, and who treats your beloved companion with respect.

The first thing to do when looking for a veterinarian is to check with other dog owners whose opinion you value. Ask friends, relatives, cowork-

Regular veterinary care, coupled with a healthy diet and regular exercise, will give your pet a longer lifespan and greater quality of life.

ers, or Rottweiler breeders whether they can recommend a veterinarian. Ask what they like about their vets. Are the prices reasonable? Is it fairly easy to get an appointment? Does the veterinary hospital have convenient hours?

You can also request a recommendation from the American Animal Hospital Association (AAHA.) The AAHA is the only companion animal veterinarian association in the United States. This organization has established high standards of quality for veterinarians and facilities. Vets who are members of the AAHA meet these standards, and their facilities are regularly inspected by the organization.

When you've identified a few good prospects, call the veterinarians' offices to get additional information. You'll want to find out what they charge for routine veterinary care, such as annual exams, vaccinations, and spaying or neutering surgery. Ask how the vet handles off-hour emergency cases—is the office open on

evenings and weekends, or is there an emergency clinic nearby to handle such situations?

The next step is to meet prospective veterinarians in person. Some things you'll want to keep in mind include: Does the veterinarian treat you and your dog with kindness and respect? Does the veterinarian explain things to you in terms you can understand? Does the veterinarian take the time to answer your questions and address your concerns? Does the veterinarian have experience with the Rottweiler breed? Don't forget to also evaluate the courtesy and professionalism of the staff—they're all a part of the health care package. After considering all these factors, you'll be able to

Ask prospective veterinarians how much experience they have with large-breed dogs like Rottweilers.

make an informed decision about your dog's veterinary care. This will give you considerable peace of mind.

THE FIRST VETERINARY EXAM

Regardless of where you obtained your Rottweiler, or whether you purchased a puppy or adopted an adult dog, you should schedule your dog's first veterinary appointment immediately after bringing your new companion home. You'll want to determine your dog's health status as soon as possible, before your heartstrings have grown too strong or health guarantees have expired. Schedule this exam within 24 to 48 hours after you bring your Rottweiler home.

Be prepared before this initial veterinarian visit. Bring any documentation you have received with regard to your dog's medical history. The breeder or shelter may have provided you with information about your dog's vaccinations, medications, treatments, or neuter or spay sur-

gery. This data will help the vet determine your dog's needs. It's also a good idea to write down any questions you may have concerning your dog's growth and development, behaviors, or health, so you won't forget to ask the veterinarian about them. Finally, bring along a stool sample, so the veterinarian can determine whether your dog is plagued by internal parasites.

During the exam, the veterinarian will check your dog's gums and teeth, eyes, and ears. She should check your dog's heart and lungs with a stethoscope. She should palpate your dog's abdomen to feel for any abnormalities. She might also draw a finger against the lay of your dog's fur to check his skin and coat condition. And if she's really good, she might even evaluate your Rottweiler's gait to check for any signs of hip dysplasia.

VACCINATIONS

Your dog's first veterinary exam is also a time when your veterinarian will recommend any vaccinations your dog may need. Vaccinations that are recommended for all dogs are called "core" vaccines. These protect your dog from very common, highly contagious, and extremely serious viruses. There are other vaccines, considered "non-core," that

FAST FACT

When choosing a veterinarian, narrow your choices down to those vets within a reasonable driving distance from your home. You don't want to drive too far in the case of an emergency.

are recommended only for dogs in high-risk situations.

CANINE ADENOVIRUS: There are two forms of this virus. Canine Adenovirus-1 is responsible for causing infectious canine hepatitis, a disease that attacks a dog's liver and kidneys. The resulting jaundice leads to a yellowish shading of the skin or eyes. It can also cause swelling of the belly. Canine Adenovirus-2 causes a mild respiratory illness that is not exceptionally harmful by itself, but can cause problems if a dog is already sick.

Although there is a vaccine for Canine Adenovirus-1, it is not recommended because of the side effects it causes. The vaccine for Canine Adenovirus-2, which provides adequate protection against both forms of the virus, is a "core" vaccine that should be a part of every dog's routine health care.

DISTEMPER: A highly contagious viral disease, distemper is most often fatal for puppies, though it can also kill adult dogs. The disease causes discharge of the eyes and nose, fever, vomiting, diarrhea, and severe lethargy. At some point in their lives, almost all dogs will be exposed to the virus that causes distemper, and there is no cure for the disease. This is why it's imperative that you vaccinate your Rottweiler.

KENNEL COUGH: Kennel cough is a highly contagious respiratory condition characterized by a dry, hacking cough. It is caused primarily by the bacterium *Bordetella bronchiseptica*, often in combination with the parainfluenza and Canine Adenovirus-2 viruses. The intranasal Bordetella vaccine protects against all three agents. Since kennel cough is commonly spread among dogs housed in groups, vaccination is recommended for any dog that comes in contact with other dogs—for example, in training classes or at dog shows.

LEPTOSPIROSIS: A bacterial infection that affects the liver and kidneys, leptospirosis produces symptoms of fever, jaundice, and excessive water consumption. The vaccine for leptospirosis is not considered a core vaccine, and vaccination may only be necessary in areas where outbreaks have occurred. Nevertheless, some veterinarians consider the symptoms worrisome enough to warrant vaccination as a precaution.

LYME DISEASE: Lyme disease is a bacterial infection transmitted by ticks. The symptoms can vary greatly from one individual to another but often include stiffness, lameness, swelling of the joints, swelling or redness at the site of the tick bite, and general malaise. The Lyme disease vaccine is recommended for any dog that lives in or travels to areas where ticks are present.

PARAINFLUENZA: Like a human flu virus, canine parainfluenza causes respiratory symptoms such as coughing and nasal discharge. While parainfluenza is usually not deadly by itself, it is highly contagious and can lead to pneumonia or a weakened immune system, which is why many veterinarians recommend vaccination.

PARVOVIRUS: Parvovirus is another potentially fatal disease that is most dangerous for puppies. It affects the gastrointestinal system and can cause bloody diarrhea, high fevers, vomiting, and lethargy. Dogs that survive the disease can be left with permanent damage. The parvovirus vaccine can keep your dog safe.

RABIES: Rabies is a viral disease that attacks the brain. Infected wildlife can transmit this disease to dogs through a bite and other forms of contact. Humans can also be infected with rabies. This disease is almost always fatal to dogs, and if untreated it is also fatal to humans. Animals

that have contracted rabies will die within 10 days of being infected. Initial symptoms include fever, restlessness, aggressiveness, foaming at the mouth, lethargy, mania, and paralysis. Infected animals may also be sensitive to light. By law, all dogs in North America must have rabies vaccinations, though the protocols vary by municipality and state. Your veterinarian can tell you what the rabies requirements are for your area.

PARASITE CONTROL

Viruses and bacterium are not the only enemies to your Rottweiler's health. Parasites can lurk insidiously inside or outside of your dog's body, some so small they are invisible to the naked eye. These tiny creatures can have a serious impact on your dog's health.

EXTERNAL PARASITES

Fleas are the most common and annoying external parasites. These creatures subsist on the blood of a host animal, and can cause a tremendous amount of discomfort. Intense itching can lead to skin damage from scratching. In severe cases, especially with puppies, fleas can cause life-threatening anemia. Fleas also transmit tapeworms to pets.

Always address any flea problem immediately, as a small infestation

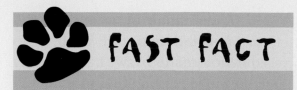

FAST FACT

A few fleas can become a major infestation in a very short time. A female flea can produce up to 2,000 eggs in just a few weeks!

can quickly become into a parasitic nightmare. Preventive treatments are highly recommended in warmer climates where fleas proliferate easily. If your dog gets fleas, you'll have to treat all the pets in your household, as well as your home and yard, in order to get the problem under control. Many flea-eradication products are available; always be careful to follow the directions and make sure that the products you use are safe for all the pets in your household. If you have difficulties getting rid of an infestation, consult your veterinarian. She will be able to recommend an effective plan of action.

A fine-toothed pet comb can be used to remove fleas and their eggs from your dog's coat.

Ticks are another type of external parasite. They are round, flat, spider-like creatures that tend to prefer the blood-rich areas of a dog's neck and ears. While ticks don't cause much physical discomfort for their hosts, they are capable of transmitting a number of diseases to our canine friends. If you live in an area where ticks thrive, minimize your dog's exposure by keeping him out of tall grass during tick season—usually from late spring through summer. Check your shorthaired Rottweiler daily for ticks by giving him a thorough petting and investigating any small lumps you feel. Remove any ticks you find by grasping them close to their heads with tweezers and pulling them off quickly. Afterward, be sure to disinfect your hands, the tweezers, and the bite site.

There are a number of very effective topical products you can use to kill and repel ticks. These are usually applied to a spot of skin on your dog's back. An added benefit of these treatments is that they can also provide protection against fleas.

Not all external parasites are visible to the naked eye, as are ticks and fleas. A number of mite species can proliferate unseen on your pet's skin. If you notice any patchy hair loss, itching, skin irritation, poor coat condition, or flaky skin, always take

Some of the diseases transmitted to dogs from ticks include Lyme disease, ehrlichiosis, Rocky Mountain spotted fever, and tick paralysis. Always remove ticks promptly and use a tick preventative if possible.

your dog to the veterinarian for a proper diagnosis. Damage caused by external parasites is easier to remedy when your dog gets prompt treatment.

Demodex mites, which normally exist on dogs, occasionally overpopulate and cause demodectic mange. This condition is thought to be

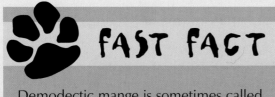

FAST FACT

Demodectic mange is sometimes called "red mange" due to the red, inflamed skin it typically causes.

caused by an immature immune system and is often outgrown as a young dog matures. Still, its effects can become serious enough to require treatment.

Sarcoptic mites cause sarcoptic mange, a much more serious and contagious type of mange. Treatment often consists of multiple applications of insecticidal dips or sprays. The prognosis is best when the condition is treated before it becomes too advanced.

INTERNAL PARASITES

Intestinal parasites that can afflict your Rottweiler include roundworms (which are the most common), hookworms, whipworms, and tapeworms. All have complicated life cycles that eventually culminate in an adult stage inside the dog's intestine. Puppies can acquire intestinal worms from their mother's milk or, in some cases, before they are even born. Adult dogs can pick up intestinal worms in a number of ways—from the soil, from an infected animal's feces, or from ingesting the carcass of a wild animal. In the case of tapeworms, they are transmitted to dogs by fleas. Some visible external symptoms of a worm infestation include a bloated belly, lethargy, diarrhea, and an inability to grow properly, especially for puppies.

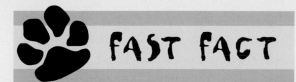

FAST FACT

More than 90 percent of puppies are infected with intestinal worms. They can acquire worms from their mothers before they are born, or through their mother's milk.

An annual fecal exam by your veterinarian can help detect the presence of intestinal worms in your dog; the vet will determine the appropriate treatment. Be aware that not all worming treatments are effective against all types of worms. Tapeworms, in particular, require specialized treatment.

Heartworms are another worm-type parasite. This deadly invader, which is spread by mosquitoes, targets the cardiopulmonary systems of dogs. The adult worms can grow to 6 inches (15 cm) in length within a dog's heart and multiply to the point of causing serious cardiac distress and eventually death. Any dog that lives in areas where mosquitoes reside should receive regular heartworm preventives.

COMMON HEALTH PROBLEMS

Every breed of dog is prone to certain health problems, and Rottweilers are no exception. You should be aware of the symptoms and treatment for these disorders, as well as the availability of genetic testing for conditions that are genetically inherited.

BLOAT: Bloat is a problem that occurs in larger dog breeds, like Rottweilers. When a dog gulps air while swallowing food or water, gulps air after vigorous exercise, or eats inappropriate items like yeast, the dog's stomach can fill with gas, swell, and become distended. The bloated stomach presses against internal organs, restricting their function and creating a painful and terrifying situation for the dog. Bloat may develop into a life-threatening condition known as torsion, or Gastric Dilatation-Volvulus, in which the stomach twists and nothing can get into or out of it. Carbon dioxide builds up in the blood because the internal abdominal pressure prevents the dog's heart and lungs from doing their jobs of cleansing and oxygenating the blood. As a result, the dog's blood pressure drops, his body becomes toxic, and the stomach continues to become painfully distended. If this occurs, you must seek immediate veterinary care, as bloat and torsion can kill your Rottweiler in less than an hour.

Symptoms of bloat include unsuccessful attempts to vomit, increased anxiety and restlessness, and a swollen abdomen that may feel tight like a drum. Your Rottweiler will probably not act like himself, and may curl into a ball and whine or lick his stomach because he is so uncomfortable.

To prevent bloat, feed your dog several small meals a day so he does not wolf down his food out of hunger. One helpful technique is to soak your dog's kibble in water for five minutes before you feed it to him; this causes the kibble to expand outside of his stomach, rather than inside. In addition, keep your dog's water bowl full so he doesn't become so thirsty that he feels compelled to gulp down the water when the bowl is finally filled. Also, avoid exercising your Rottweiler for at least an hour before and two hours after feeding time.

EYE DISORDERS: Several hereditary problems can affect your Rottweiler's vision. Cataracts, distichiasis, entropion, and progressive retinal atrophy have all been known to occur in this breed. If you notice any irritation or abnormality of your dog's eye, have your veterinarian check it immediately. Eye problems can become worse very quickly, so prompt treatment is the best approach.

Cataracts are opaque obstructions that form in the eye lens. Some cataracts remain relatively small and

This female Rottweiler's eyes have a milky white appearance, which dog owners sometimes mistake as a sign of cataracts. The whiteness is actually caused by a natural hardening of the lens due to age. Cataracts cause more obvious opaque spots in the lens.

create minimal barriers to vision. Others can result in blindness. Surgery is the only effective treatment for cataracts. In severe cases the diseased lens can be replaced with an artificial one, but this procedure requires the expertise of a veterinary ophthalmologist and is quite expensive.

Distichiasis is a hereditary condition that involves the growth of abnormal hairs on the eyelid. When these hairs grow into and rub against the eye, they can cause injury and vision-reducing scarring. Mild cases may not require treatment, but if eye injury occurs, surgery is required to correct the condition.

Entropion is another hereditary condition that affects the eyelid. Dogs with this condition have eyelids that roll inward, causing the eyelashes to abrade the cornea. As with distichiasis, injury and scarring to the cornea can result in vision impairment. Young dogs with this condition may have their eyelids "tacked" into the correct position so they will grow normally. Older dogs may require surgery to correct the problem.

Unfortunately, Rottweilers are known to suffer from several disorders of the retina, the light-sensitive tissue inside the eye. These include progressive retinal atrophy, retinal detachment, and retinal dysplasia.

All three conditions result in total, permanent blindness and cannot be cured. Currently, there is no genetic test available to detect these disorders, so it is crucially important to ask your breeder whether her breeding stock has any history of these conditions.

PIGMENTATION DISORDERS: Some Rottweilers are affected by pigment disorders that rob their skin of color. Hypopigmentation is a lack of pigment on the nose and lips. Vitiligo causes patches of skin to lose pigment, and can also cause your Rottweiler's hair in these areas to turn white. Neither of these conditions causes any discomfort for the dog, although they will disqualify your Rottweiler from conformation shows. Hypopigmentation and

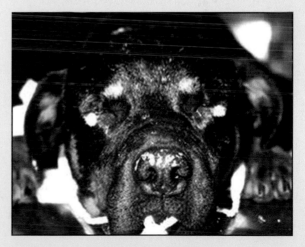

The white patches on this Rottweiler's face indicate the skin disorder Vitiligo.

Vitiligo are autoimmune disorders, in which the body's own immune system attacks the color-producing cells in the skin for some reason. There is no cure, but dogs with these conditions can live normal and happy lives.

ENDOCRINE DISORDERS: Endocrine disorders affect many purebred dog breeds, including the Rottweiler. It is the responsibility of various glands to produce a balanced mix of hormones to keep a dog's body functioning properly. When this balance is disrupted, it can cause symptoms like lethargy, vomiting, diarrhea, hair loss, or lack of appetite.

Hypoadrenocorticism, also called Addison's disease, is caused when the adrenal glands do not produce enough of substances called glucocorticoid and mineralocorticoid. These substances are necessary for the body to function properly. A blood test is the only way to diagnose this condition with certainty. Although Addison's disease can be fatal if left untreated, the hormone deficiency can easily be corrected with supplements.

Hypothyroidism occurs when the thyroid gland does not produce enough thyroid hormone. This condition is often caused when the dog's own immune system attacks the thyroid gland and diminishes its ability

to function properly. Some unusual symptoms associated with hypothyroidism include weight gain and intolerance to cold temperatures. Treatment consists of oral supplements to increase the thyroid hormone to its proper level.

ORTHOPEDIC DISORDERS: Rottweilers, like other large dog breeds, are prone to hip dysplasia and elbow dysplasia. Both conditions involve joints that have developed abnormally. Hip dysplasia is a malformation of the hip socket and/or the head of the femur (the thigh bone) of the rear legs. Elbow dysplasia results when a small bone in the front leg fails to fuse properly during puppyhood. Both abnormalities can

FAST FACT

Large dogs like Rottweilers can occasionally experience a "rapid growth" disorder called eosinophilic panosteitis, which is an inflammatory bone disease that causes significant pain. If this is a problem for your puppy, you'll have to discuss dietary options with your veterinarian, because the high calorie content in puppy food may exacerbate the problem. Although there is no cure, you can take steps to keep your puppy comfortable until he outgrows this condition.

Rottweilers are prone to overheating during hot weather. When the temperature rises, be careful not to overwork your dog. On particularly hot days, your Rottweiler will appreciate the opportunity to cool off under a lawn sprinkler or in a kiddie wading pool.

be crippling and painful or just uncomfortable, depending on how much the bone is deformed and whether bone rubs against bone whenever the dog moves. In many cases surgery can relieve the pain and lameness that result from hip and elbow dysplasia, allowing the dog to live a more normal life. Overfeeding and excessive exercise can both worsen these conditions, so it's best to keep pups on the lean side and be sensible about exercise.

Dysplasia is hereditary, so responsible breeders always x-ray their dogs' hips and elbows before they decide whether to breed them. The x-rays are sent to the Orthopedic Foundation for Animals for evaluation, and the dog's owner can use the results to decide whether her dog is sound enough to breed. As the practice of x-raying dogs for dysplasia before breeding them has grown more common, the incidence of these disorders has begun to diminish. However, because of the complex genetic blueprint for dysplasia, it's unlikely that x-ray evaluation of breeding stock will ever completely eradicate these disorders.

❧❧❧

Ensuring your Rottweiler's good health will help your dog maintain the image he was born to have—one of strength, vigor, and heartiness.

CHAPTER SEVEN

Enjoying Your Rottweiler

Your Rottweiler is an exceptionally talented and athletic fellow. There are many ways you can enjoy your new pet to the fullest. You'll probably find that additional time spent training your pet enriches both of your lives immensely.

ADVANCED TRAINING

Training is one of the most rewarding activities you can do with your Rottweiler. Training builds trust. It increases communication and strengthens the human-canine bond. Perhaps most important, proper

Your Rottweiler will be happy to participate in practically any outdoor activity—as long as it means he's spending time with you.

training will give you a more responsive, better-behaved companion. Of course, the greatest benefit is that it's just plain fun!

AKC Canine Good Citizen: In its efforts to promote responsible dog ownership and the acceptance of dogs as good citizens, the American Kennel Club offers certification for any dog that passes the AKC Canine Good Citizen (CGC) test. This test is also the foundation of training for dogs approved for therapy work through Therapy Dogs International (TDI).

To earn a CGC certificate, dogs are tested on basic obedience and social skills. The dog owners are evaluated on the care and appearance of their dogs, as well as their appropriate handling of their dogs.

Many dog-training facilities now offer training classes to work on CGC skills. You can enroll in a class or teach the skills to your dog on your own, but an approved CGC evaluator must administer the test. For a complete list of test skills, or to locate an evaluator in your area, visit the AKC Web site at www.akc.org.

Obedience: If you want to take your dog's training to a higher level, obedience competition is another wonderful activity. Your intelligent Rottweiler has plenty of potential in this department. You'll have to enroll in training classes, as your Rottweiler will need to learn some very specialized skills to succeed in obedience competitions.

The American Kennel Club sponsors obedience trials at various levels of difficulty, with opportunities to earn titles as your dog proceeds through each level. Even at the novice level, mastering the skill set can be challenging. Your dog will have to learn to heel on and off leash, obey the "stay" command while in a group of dogs, and stand for examination, in addition to other basic obedience commands. When your dog executes these skills adequately, he'll earn a Companion Dog (CD) title. This entitles you to include the designation "CD" after your purebred Rottweiler's registered name.

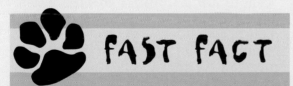

FAST FACT

The AKC Canine Good Citizen (CGC) program has become so popular that other countries have used it as a model to start their own programs, such as the Kennel Club's Good Citizen Dog Scheme in Britain.

Titles earned in obedience are customarily listed in their abbreviated form after a dog's registered name. Other obedience titles include Companion Dog Excellent (CDX), which is offered at the open level; and Utility Dog (UD) and Utility Dog Excellent (UDX), which are earned at the utility level. If you are really ambitious, you can continue to compete at the utility level to gain points toward the coveted Obedience Trial Champion (OTCh) title.

If the benefits of obedience competition appeal to you, but you'd prefer to participate in a slightly less disciplined sport, you might want to consider AKC Rally obedience. This sport consists of a course with 10 to 20 stations, each of which has a sign that indicates which obedience skill must be performed. Dogs that record high scores can earn AKC titles in this sport, also. For more information on getting started in any type of AKC obedience competition, visit the American Kennel Club's Web site.

CANINE SPORTS AND ACTIVITIES

Rottweilers can excel at, and earn titles in, many types of activities other than obedience competitions. Some of the activities for which Rottweilers tend to have a lot of passion include agility trials, Schutzhund tests, tracking competitions, weight pulls, and search-and-rescue work.

Regardless of which canine activities appeal to you, keep in mind that your dog will have has own preferences. Observe your Rottweiler to see what kinds of activities really excite him. Your dog's enthusiasm may convince you to pursue a sport you hadn't considered. If you have the energy and motivation, there is no reason you can't train your Rottweiler in more than one sport.

AGILITY: Agility is a fast-paced sport that requires participants to race through a course consisting of various jumps, weave poles, tunnels, ramps, and other obstacles. The goal is to complete the course in the fastest time with the fewest penalties for faults. Agility can be a great way to provide exercise and mental stimulation to a canine companion.

There are a number of organizations that sanction agility trials in the United States, including the American Kennel Club, the United States Dog Agility Association (USDAA), and the North American Dog Agility Council (NADAC). The titles vary, depending on the organization that issues them, but all of these organizations offer progressively difficult levels of competition.

Although it will take some time to teach your dog how to handle each of these obstacles, your Rottweiler will appreciate the opportunity to use his physical gifts. The easiest way to learn how to train your dog for the sport is to enroll in an agility training class. You and your dog can practice negotiating agility obstacles in your backyard. To find out about upcoming competitions in your area, check with your training instructor or visit the Web sites of agility organizations.

SCHUTZHUND AND WORKING DOG SPORT: Schutzhund, which means "protection dog" in German, was a test developed in the early 1900s to determine whether a dog was suited for police work. The purpose of this was to help breeders choose the dogs with the most useful traits for their breeding programs. The Schutzhund test evaluates a dog's aptitude for obedience, tracking, and protection—all areas in which the Rottweiler excels—as well as the dog's courage, intelligence, desire to work, and trainability.

The requirements for Schutzhund are so demanding that training isn't enough. Dogs must pass a temperament test before they are allowed to participate. Those dogs that are found to be stable, trustworthy and

Agility trials are fun for both Rottweilers and their owners.

controllable can compete at three levels of difficulty. In Schutzhund competitions, dogs must demonstrate obedience skills both on and off leash, follow scent tracks, jump hurdles, scale a six-foot-tall slanted wall, and pursue and hold a "villain" at bay.

If you are interested in becoming involved in this type of activity, it is

Novice Rottweiler owners should not attempt to train their dog for Schutzhund; instead, look for a professional trainer who is experienced in this discipline, or enroll in a Schutzhund training class in your area.

very important to first learn as much as possible and seek the guidance of those more experienced. As you can imagine, teaching a large, powerful Rottweiler how to use his teeth to subdue a criminal is not an endeavor to be taken lightly. Attempting to train your dog without proper knowledge will only create a dangerous animal. When training is done properly, however, you can turn your Rottweiler into a very controllable

and trustworthy working dog.

The Deutscher Berband der Gebrauchshundsportvereine (DVG) is a German organization that governs the sport of Schutzhund throughout the world. You can find out about Schutzhund competitions in the United States by visiting the organization's Web site at www.dvgamerica.com.

In 2006, the American Kennel Club sanctioned its own version of this activity, called Working Dog Sport. Like Schutzhund, Working Dog Sport requires a temperament test and offers three levels of competition. The AKC provides an online regulations handbook on Working Dog Sport, in PDF format, at http://www.akc.org/pdfs/rulebooks/RES600.pdf.

TRACKING: If you are impressed by your dog's sense of smell and love the outdoors, you and your Rottweiler may enjoy tracking competitions. Tracking is a challenging sport that requires endurance and physical strength, as scent tracks may go through rugged terrain at times. One thing that makes tracking competitions different from other canine sports is that your dog does not compete directly against other dogs. This is strictly a pass-or-fail test. If your dog completes the track, you'll have a title to add to his name. As a result, there is often a lot of camaraderie among tracking participants, as many want to see everyone succeed.

The three different levels of this sport offer progressively difficult tracks. The three tracking titles that can be earned include Tracking Dog (for following a 440-to-500-yard track with several turns), Tracking Dog Excellent (for following a 1,000-yard track with several turns), and Variable Surface Tracking (for following a scent over three different surfaces on an 800-yard track).

Flyball is another dog sport that's fun to watch. Flyball events require dogs to race through a course, leap over hurdles, and press a lever on a box so that a tennis ball pops out. The dog catches the ball and races back to his handler. Teams of four dogs compete, with the fastest team winning.

If you want to explore your Rottweiler's talent for tracking, visit the AKC's Web site at www.akc.org for a complete list of rules. Some of the best resources on tracking include the books *Mastering Variable Surface Tracking* by Ed Presnall (Dogwise Publishing, 2004) and *Tracking Dog: Theory and Methods* by Glen R. Johnson (Barkleigh Productions, 2003).

WEIGHT PULL COMPETITIONS: If you'd like to test the strength of your Rottweiler, consider the challenge of weight pull competitions. In this sport, dogs of different breeds compete against other dogs that are about the same size. Each dog in the class takes a turn pulling a weighted sled or wheeled cart over a 16 foot (4.9 m) distance while their owners urge them on. Dogs that fail to move the weight within 60 seconds or stop pulling before they've reached the 16-foot mark are eliminated. The weight on the sled or cart is then increased, and dogs that have completed the first pull compete again. The dog that pulls the heaviest weight in the shortest amount of time is the winner.

To prepare your dog for competition, he'll need to know basic obedience skills so you can control him in the pulling chute. You will not be

Because of their strength and endurance, some Rottweilers excel at weight pull competitions.

allowed to touch your dog once he starts pulling. He'll also have to become accustomed to wearing a special harness and pulling heavy loads. Once you get your dog started in this activity, one fun way to practice could be to have him pull you on a sled, skis, or roller skates!

There are several organizations that hold weight pull competitions in the United States, including the United Pulling Federation (www.upfweightpull.webs.com) and the International Weight Pull Association (www.iwpa.net). You can learn more about getting started in this sport by visiting their Web sites.

SEARCH AND RESCUE: If you want to participate in an activity that can help others, search and rescue (SAR) is a good choice. A search-and-rescue dog is trained to follow his nose to help people in trouble. The demands of this activity are extremely high. The greatest toll is perhaps the

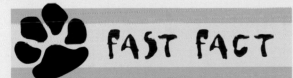

FAST FACT

Canine athletes are just as prone to injuries as human athletes. Condition your Rottweiler gradually to handle the rigors of canine sports, and treat injuries promptly.

FAST FACT

Some Rottweilers have a very nurturing disposition. If you think your well-behaved Rottweiler might be a good candidate for therapy dog work, visit the website for Therapy Dogs International (www.tdi-dogs.org) or the Delta Society (www.deltasociety.org) for information about becoming involved in this sort of activity.

emotions a search can evoke. From the supreme joy of finding a lost child to the despair of a natural disaster's aftermath, search-and-rescue work can be psychologically draining.

This type of volunteer work also requires a significant commitment of time and expense. It can take up to a year to train a search-and-rescue dog, and this training must be conducted on a regular basis to keep the dog's skills intact. The dog's handler also has to be educated in proper protocols and safety procedures in order to perform this difficult job. In addition, search-and-rescue volunteers often wind up paying for specialized equipment and travel. Before you get involved, determine whether you have the time and financial resources to invest in this endeavor.

If you decide that you are truly passionate about search and rescue, your Rottweiler may make a great partner. To find our more, check the Web site of the National Association for Search and Rescue (NASAR) at www.nasar.org. It should be able to guide you to a search-and-rescue group in your area.

SHOWING YOUR ROTTWEILER

If your purebred Rottweiler has champion show dogs in his lineage, there is a good chance he can succeed in conformation competition. It only takes a few wins for some people to become hopelessly addicted to dog shows. For a dog lover, there is no thrill greater than seeing your pride-and-joy become a champion.

Dog showing can be an expensive proposition. First, there is the often-substantial cost of a good-quality show dog. There are entry fees and travel expenses. You may also have to pay handler fees and training fees.

Before you become involved in showing, you should do plenty of research. Study the Rottweiler breed standard, and attend several dog shows so you can learn how they are run. The best way to get the training and practice you'll need is to enroll your Rottweiler in a conformation training class and participate in a few "fun matches." Training classes will give you the benefit of expert instruction while teaching your dog

DOG SHOW GROOMING

Grooming is one aspect of showing that will make you glad you chose a Rottweiler. Unlike some other dog breeds, Rottweilers don't require hours of preparation before a show. This doesn't mean you can simply walk into a show ring with your dog and expect to succeed, however. You'll still have to learn the unique grooming techniques that apply to this breed, such as how to treat "hot spots" (thin or bald spots) or other coat imperfections and how to maintain your Rottweiler's nails at the "short-short" length expected of show dogs.

At first, it helps to work with a mentor who can instruct you in many of the fine details of grooming and showing. This could be your dog's breeder, or it could be a member of a local Rottweiler club. Search the American Rottweiler Club (ARC) Web site at www.amrottclub.org for a list of Rottweiler clubs in your area.

how to behave in the company of other dogs. Fun matches don't provide points toward championships, but they provide an excellent education for show dogs. Check the AKC website for a schedule of fun matches in your area.

BREEDING YOUR ROTTWEILER

It doesn't make much sense to promote your dog's superior qualities in the show ring if you do not wish to pass on those marvelous traits to subsequent generations. This is why show dogs are required to be kept intact (not neutered or spayed). You must be willing to accept the challenges that come with owning an intact dog and take precautions to prevent your pet from roaming or producing accidental litters.

Breeding should never be done with the goal of earning back the money you paid for your Rottweiler.

If you are interested in breeding a purebred Rottweiler, then do it responsibly. This means you should purchase quality breeding stock, learn about genetics, and have your dog tested for genetic defects. Responsible breeders do not breed for "fun," just to have a litter of puppies that may eventually end up populating animal shelters and rescues that are already overflowing. They breed for one reason only—to improve the Rottweiler breed. If you are not committed to this honorable goal, it's better to leave breeding to people who are.

You should be motivated by a genuine love of the breed. Responsible breeders rarely turn a profit—in fact, most barely break even when all the costs are considered.

Breeding, whelping, and raising a litter of puppies is a lot of work. It can also be very expensive. You will need to pay for genetic testing to find out whether your Rottweiler is a suitable candidate for breeding. If you have a female dog, you may have other veterinary expenses that result from prenatal care or birthing complications. Raising puppies isn't cheap either. Puppies need veterinary exams, vaccinations, and worming medication. They also need to be weaned, fed, and socialized before going to their new homes.

In short, breeding a dog is not a simple matter of pairing males and females together and letting nature take its course. It involves the science of genetics and requires a joint effort from you, your veterinarian, and probably another dog owner. Lots of research and planning are required before you should consider plunging into this pool. If breeding is really something you'd like to do, be prepared to learn as much as you can.

TRAVELING WITH YOUR ROTTWEILER

Traveling with a pet can be a pleasure or a pain, depending on how well you prepare for the trip. Take the stress out of traveling by being prepared. Start with a travel list of everything you'll need to pack for your Rottweiler. You might even want to give your pet a travel bag of his own. That way, it will be easier to keep track of his things and keep them organized.

CANINE TRAVEL LIST

Bed	Dog food	Toys
Bottled water	Food and water dishes	Treats
Brush	ID tag	Vaccination records
Collar	Leash	Your veterinarian's
Crate	Medications	phone number
Current photo of	Moist wipes	Waste bags
your dog	Tie-out	

Basic care items include food, leash, dishes, grooming supplies, waste bags so you can clean up after your pet, and toys to keep him happy. You'll also want to bring documentation of his vaccinations (especially the rabies shot) and your veterinarian's phone number. You never know when an emergency might require your dog's health information. Also, bring along a description and current photo of your dog just in case he becomes lost while you're away.

If you plan to stay at a hotel or motel, always make lodging arrangements ahead of time and ask whether the hotel is pet friendly. It won't be a very pleasant trip if you have to drive all over an unfamiliar place trying to find lodging that accepts dogs. Some pet-friendly hotels offer a discount for dogs that have achieved the AKC Canine Good Citizen certification.

Always keep your dog's safety and comfort in mind when you are setting off on a new adventure. Never leave him unattended in a vehicle, especially in warm climates. Dogs can become frightened or disoriented when away from their home territory, so always keep your Rottweiler on a leash or tie-out when he is in an unfamiliar environment. Finally, don't forget to give your traveling companion

If you prepare properly in advance, there is no reason your Rottweiler can't accompany you on vacations.

opportunities to stretch his legs and take a potty break once in a while.

LEAVING YOUR ROTTWEILER AT HOME

When you can't take your Rottweiler with you, you'll need to arrange for his care. It's best to choose a caregiver you trust, so you'll have peace of mind, not sleepless nights, while you're gone. For short absences of a day or two, you might find a dog-loving neighbor, relative, or friend to look after your dog. For longer absences, however, you may want to hire a professional. Some professional pet sitters will come to your home several times a day to care for your dog. Others provide pet sitting services in their own homes. This may be more desirable if your dog requires the extra time and attention.

Always evaluate a prospective pet sitter carefully. A professional pet sitter will set up an initial appointment with you to meet your Rottweiler and discuss the dog's needs. The sitter should have a contract outlining services offered, be insured and bonded, and be a member of a professional organization such as the

National Association of Professional Pet Sitters (NAPPS) or Pet Sitters International (PSI).

Pay attention to how the sitter responds to your dog. Does the sitter seem knowledgeable about dogs and ask a lot of questions about your dog? Most important, does your dog feel comfortable with the sitter? Because Rottweilers are rather territorial, your dog may not like having a stranger enter his home in your absence. However, Rottweilers often decide rather quickly whether or not they trust someone. You may need to schedule a mock visit to make sure your Rottweiler sees the pet sitter as a care provider rather than an interloper. If you have any doubts, look for another sitter.

CANINE FIRST AID KIT

Rottweilers are great camping and hiking companions, but be sure to bring a first aid kit. It should contain the following items:

Aspirin* (for pain relief)
Bandage scissors
Benadryl* (for severe bee stings or allergic reactions)
Eye wash
First aid tape
Gauze pads (different sizes)

Gauze rolls
Muzzle (or strip of cloth or rope)
Pet first aid manual
Styptic (clotting) powder
Triple antibiotic ointment
Tweezers (for removing ticks or splinters)
Vet wrap bandages

*Obtain dosage instructions from your veterinarian

Depending on your situation, a boarding kennel might be a better choice than a dog sitter. Today, the typical kennel is much more than a cold, hard doggy jail. Many kennels now offer soft bedding, toys, group playtime with other dogs, special feeding arrangements, and other amenities. Some boarding kennels house their charges in small, individual rooms instead of in kennel cages. They may offer a whole menu of optional services, including individual playtime with humans, group playtime with other dogs, canine massage, and even aromatherapy.

Depending on how much you're willing to pay, you can arrange for your dog to have his own luxury vacation. But regardless of how great they seem in their ads or over the phone, you should evaluate boarding facilities in person with the same scrutiny as you would a pet sitter. Are the facilities clean? Is soft bedding provided? Do the operators show an interest in your dog, or will your dog be treated like just another boarder? Obey your instincts, for if you have bad feelings they are sure to haunt you during your travels.

CARING FOR YOUR SENIOR ROTTWEILER

As you journey through life with a Rottweiler, you'll become aware that in many ways, dogs get better with age. The folly of youth is replaced by quiet obedience. The energetic escapades of adulthood are replaced with placid devotion. Unfortunately, not all age-related changes are positive. The effect on your dog's body may not be as desirable as the effects on his temperament.

The average Rottweiler lives nine to ten years, but you will begin to see signs of aging when he's around seven years old. One of the most obvious changes will be stiffness in his limbs and joints. Arthritis is very common in older dogs, but it does not have to result in a life of pain. Make sure your senior dog receives regular, low-impact exercise to keep his joints flexible. An orthopedic dog bed can provide comfort, and your veterinarian can recommend supplements or prescribe pain medication if the condition becomes severe.

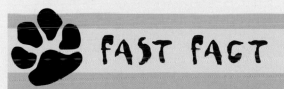

Adult Rottweilers should receive annual veterinary exams, but the American Animal Hospital Association (AAHA) recommends that senior dogs be examined about every six months. This can help ensure that age-related health problems are diagnosed and treated early.

Your senior Rottweiler may also suffer from diminishing senses, although you probably won't notice unless a deficiency becomes pronounced. Dogs tend to adjust to these types of changes gracefully. Eyesight can dim, hearing can become less acute, and even your dog's sense of taste might decline. If you do notice any of these changes, you can take steps to accommodate your Rottweiler. For example, if your dog seems to have trouble seeing well, avoid moving furniture around in his home to keep him from becoming confused and disoriented. If your dog's hearing has become impaired, you can use hand signals to communicate with him. And if your dog seems to be losing his appetite due to a reduction in his sense of taste, enhance his meals with something to make the food more palatable.

Some age-related changes cause more worrisome symptoms. Your senior Rottweiler's internal functions may not be as efficient anymore. This can result in vomiting or refusal to eat due to a sensitive stomach. It can cause occasional diarrhea or frequent urination. It can manifest in a poor skin and coat condition, lack of energy, poor circulation, or a host of other symptoms. Always discuss such symptoms with your veterinarian, as many of the conditions that cause them are treatable.

SPECIAL DIETS AND WEIGHT CONTROL

To treat various age-related conditions, your veterinarian may recommend changing what your dog eats. Special diets have been developed to help dogs that have heart problems or diminished kidney and liver function. There are easily digestible diets formulated to cater to sensi-

Your senior Rottweiler may begin to grow grey around his muzzle.

tive stomachs. There are even soft-food diets available for older canines that have lost some or all of their teeth.

The most common special diet is probably one used to help your senior dog lose weight. Older dogs just don't burn as many calories as they did in their younger days. You may have noticed your Rottweiler's energy level gradually decrease over the years. If you don't watch your dog's weight as he ages and adjust his food intake accordingly, your senior dog may begin to look a little too beefy. If this happens, the best course of action is to reduce the amount you feed your dog, strictly limit his treats and consumable chew products, and make sure he exercises every day.

Although prepackaged canine weight-loss diets are readily available from pet stores and on the Internet, they should only be used with a veterinarian's recommendation. This type of diet, being low in protein and carbohydrates, tends to produce unwanted side effects, such as a lower energy level, loss of muscle mass, and a dull coat.

EXERCISE

Proper diet provides only half the formula for canine fitness. The other half is exercise. Exercise is vital to prevent obesity or the loss of muscle tissue in older dogs. It

Older Rottweilers still need daily exercise, but be aware of your aging dog's limitations. Don't overdo workouts, especially on warm or humid days.

helps circulation, which distributes oxygen and nutrients to vital organs and keeps things working properly. It stimulates digestion and helps to keep old joints flexible. If you want your Rottweiler to have a good quality of life in his old age, make sure he receives a daily dose of moderate exercise.

Rottweilers that are highly driven will not need much incentive to keep active in their later years, but others may have to be coaxed off the couch. Do not allow your senior dog to overexert himself, though. When you keep your dog fit during the twilight of his life, he will have a young-at-heart attitude that will allow you to enjoy many more adventures together.

SAYING GOODBYE

It's true that old friends are the best friends, especially when it comes to dogs. But your enjoyment of your dog's senior years may be tainted with an occasional twinge of trepidation. You know that, at some point, you'll have to say goodbye. It's hard to accept the fact that dogs don't live as long as we do, but this is a sad fact of life.

Like most pet owners, you probably hope your friend will pass quietly in his sleep when it is his time, but this is not how death normally

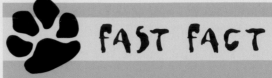

FAST FACT

Euthanasia is no longer the only end-of-life service available for dogs. Hospice-type care can keep dogs with terminal illnesses comfortable and improve their quality of life. If you're interested in this type of service, ask your veterinarian for a referral.

occurs. For many dogs, dying is a gradual and uncomfortable process. When the quality of your dog's life deteriorates to the point where your buddy is in constant pain, euthanasia may be the kindest thing you can do for him.

Your veterinarian will perform this procedure, which consists of an intravenous injection of several drugs that erase pain and suppress vital organ function. Your dog will appear to go to sleep very quickly. His heart will slow, then stop. All this occurs in just a few short minutes. It is a peaceful process, and you'll know you've done the right thing for your old friend.

COPING WITH GRIEF

Consider how you will want your dog's remains to be handled, as this may be one of the ways you find closure in your loss. Your veterinarian can assist you in evaluating the options. Although an urn or a grave marker can provide a source of remembrance, there are many other ways to preserve the priceless memories you have of your Rottweiler.

Remembering the good times can be very therapeutic, and nothing can conjure memories better than photographs. A favorite photo or a collage of photos can be framed and kept in a special place in your home. You could also plant a tree or bush in your dog's memory, or construct a garden stone that bears his name. Maybe you'd like to honor your faithful friend by doing something to benefit other dogs, like donating to a local animal shelter or a veterinary college.

Regardless of the methods you use to cope with your feelings of loss, be patient and allow your grief to subside naturally. Healing is not always measured in days or weeks—sometimes it's measured in years. If you have exceptional difficulty dealing with your loss, do not hesitate to seek the support of others. Check with local animal shelters or your veterinarian for referrals to a pet loss support group.

❧❧❧❧

From the moment you bring home an adorable black-and-rust

Looking at photos of your Rottweiler in happier times may help ease the pain of his passing.

puppy until the day you say goodbye to your venerable old friend, a Rottweiler will give you the very best he has to offer. Even his death can't take away the rich memories of the fun times that you've shared—a wealth of interest paid on a small investment of love.

Organizations to Contact

American Animal Hospital Assn.
12575 West Bayaud Ave.
Lakewood, CO 80228
Phone: 303-986-2800
Fax: 800-252-2242
E-mail: info@aahanet.org
Web site: www.aahanet.org

American Kennel Club
8051 Arco Corporate Dr., Suite 100
Raleigh, NC 27617
Phone: 919-233-9767
E-mail: info@akc.org
Web site: www.akc.org

**American Rottweiler
Association (ARC)**
Marilyn Piusz
339 Co Hwy 106
Johnstown, NY 12095-3757
Phone: 518-883-5806
Web site: www.amrottclub.org

American Working Dog Federation
Michelle Testa, Secretary
P.O. Box 25
Palmyra, VA 22955
Phone: 434-591-4552
E-mail: michelle@myrivercottage.com
Web site: www.awdf.net

Association of Pet Dog Trainers
150 Executive Center Dr., Box 35
Greenville, SC 29615
Phone: 800-738-3647
Fax: 864-331-0767
E-mail: information@apdt.com
Web site: www.apdt.com

The Canadian Kennel Club
89 Skyway Avenue, Suite 100
Etobicoke, Ontario, M9W 6R4
Canada
Phone: 416-675-5511
Fax: 416-675-6506
Web site: www.ckc.ca/en

Delta Society
875 124th Ave., NE, Suite 101
Bellevue, WA 98005
Phone: 425-226-7357
E-mail: info@deltasociety.org
Web site: www.deltasociety.org

DVG America (Schutzhund)
Sandi Purdi, Secretary
2101 S. Westmoreland Rd.
Red Oak, TX 75154
Phone: 972-617-2988
E-mail: sandidvg@att.net
Web site: www.dvgamerica.com

Humane Society of the U.S.
2100 L St., NW
Washington, DC 20037
Phone: 202-452-1100
Fax: 301-548-7701
Web site: www.hsus.org

The Kennel Club of the U.K.
1-5 Clarges St.
London W1J 8AB
United Kingdom
Phone: 0870 606 6750
Web site: www.thekennelclub.org.uk

**National Association for Search
and Rescue (NASAR)**
P.O. Box 232020
Centreville, VA 20120-2020
Phone: 703-222-6277
Web site: www.nasar.org

**National Association of Dog
Obedience Instructors**
729 Grapevine Hwy
Hurst, TX 76054-2085
E-mail: corrsec2@nadoi.org
Web site: www.nadoi.org

**National Association of
Professional Pet Sitters (NAPPS)**
17000 Commerce Parkway, Suite C
Mt. Laurel, NJ 08054
Phone: 856-439-0324
Fax: 856-439-0525
Web site: www.petsitters.org

National Dog Registry
P.O. Box 51105
Mesa, AZ 85208
Phone: 800-NDR-DOGS
Web site: www.nationaldogregistry.com

**North American Dog Agility
Council (NADAC)**
P.O. Box 1206
Colbert, OK 74733
E-mail: info@nadac.com
Web site: www.nadac.com

**North American Flyball
Association (NAFA)**
1400 West Devon Ave., #512
Chicago, IL 60660
Phone: 800-318-6312
Web site: www.flyball.org

**Orthopedic Foundation
for Animals (OFA)**
2300 East Nifong Boulevard
Columbia, MO 65201
Phone: 573-442-0418
Fax: 573-875-5073
Web site: www.offa.org

Pet Industry Joint Advisory Council
1220 19th St., NW, Suite 400
Washington, DC 20036
Phone: 202-452-1525
Fax: 202-293-4377
E-mail: info@pijac.org
Web site: www.pijac.org

Pet Loss Support Hotline
College of Veterinary Medicine
Cornell University
Ithaca, NY 14853-6401
Phone: 607-253-3932
Web site: www.vet.cornell.edu/
public/petloss

Pet Sitters International (PSI)
201 East King Street
King, NC 27021-9161
Phone: 336-983-9222
Fax: 336-983-9222
E-mail: info@petsit.com
Web site: www.petsit.com

Therapy Dogs International, Inc.
88 Bartley Road
Flanders, NJ 07836
Phone: 973-252-9800
Fax: 973-252-7171
E-mail: tdi@gti.net
Web site: www.tdi-dog.org

U.K. National Pet Register
74 North Albert St., Dept 2
Fleetwood, Lancasterhire, FY7 6BJ
United Kingdom
Web site: www.nationalpetregister.org

**United States Dog Agility
Association, Inc. (USDAA)**
P.O. Box 850955
Richardson, TX 75085-0955
Phone: 972-487-2200
Fax: 972-272-4404
E-mail: info@usdaa.com
Web site: www.usdaa.com

Veterinary Medical Databases
1717 Philo Rd.
P.O. Box 3007
Urbana, IL 61803-3007
Phone: 217-693-4800
E-mail: cerf@vmdb.org
Web site: www.vmdb.org

Further Reading

Balabanov, Ivan, and Karen Duet. *Advanced Schutzhund*. New York: Howell Book House, 1999.

Brace, Andrew. *Ultimate Rottweiler*. Lydney, England: Ringpress Books, 2003.

Eldredge, Debra. *Dog Owner's Veterinary Handbook*. New York: Howell Book House, 2007.

John, A. Meredith, and Carole L. Richards. *Raising a Champion: A Beginner's Guide to Showing Dogs*. Collingswood, N.J.: The Well Trained Dog, 2001.

Johnson, Glen R. *Tracking Dog: Theory and Methods*. Mechanicsburg, Pa.: Barkleigh Productions, 2003.

Libby, Tracy. *The Rottweiler*. Neptune City, N.J.: T.F.H. Publications, 2006.

Presnall, Ed. *Mastering Variable Surface Tracking*. Wenatchee, Wash.: Dogwise Publishing, 2004.

Internet Resources

http://www.aspca.org

The American Society for the Prevention of Cruelty to Animals provides valuable information for pet owners, including information on toxic plants from its poison control center.

http://www.petfinder.com

This website can help you find adoptable Rottweilers through shelters and rescue groups in your area.

http://www.rottnet.net

This website is devoted to Rottweiler rescue and provides resources for rescue groups and Rottweiler adopters.

http://www.usrconline.org

The United States Rottweiler Club is an organization devoted to the Rottweiler breed.

http://www.volhard.com/pages/pat.php

This web page contains information on the Puppy Aptitude Test (PAT), a personality evaluation developed by renowned dog trainers Jack and Wendy Volhard.

Index

Numbers in **bold italics** refer to captions.

Contributors

JANICE BINIOK has written numerous articles and books on companion animals, including *The Poodle* and *The Yorkshire Terrier* in Eldorado Ink's OUR BEST FRIENDS series. She has an English degree from the University of Wisconsin-Milwaukee and is a member of the Dog Writers Association of America. Janice lives on a small farm in Waukesha, Wisconsin, with her husband, two sons, and several furry family members.

Senior Consulting Editor **GARY KORSGAARD, DVM,** has had a long and distinguished career in veterinary medicine. After graduating from The Ohio State University's College of Veterinary Medicine in 1963, he spent two years as a captain in the Veterinary Corps of the U.S. Army. During that time he attended the Walter Reed Army Institute of Research and became Chief of the Veterinary Division for the Sixth Army Medical Laboratory at the Presidio, San Francisco.

In 1968 Dr. Korsgaard founded the Monte Vista Veterinary Hospital in Concord, California, where he practiced for 32 years as a small animal veterinarian. He is a past president of the Contra Costa Veterinary Association, and was one of the founding members of the Contra Costa Veterinary Emergency Clinic, serving as president and board member of that hospital for nearly 30 years.

Dr. Korsgaard retired in 2000. He enjoys golf, hiking, international travel, and spending time with his wife Susan and their three children and four grandchildren.